D0604915

The Farm

❋ ❋ ❋

The Farm

Rustic Recipes for a Year of Incredible Food

Ian Knauer

Foreword ✳ Ruth Reichl

Photography ✳ Hirsheimer & Hamilton

Houghton Mifflin Harcourt
Boston New York 2012

For information about permission to reproduce selections from this book,
write to Permissions, Houghton Mifflin Harcourt Publishing Company,
215 Park Avenue South, New York, New York 10003.

www.hmhbooks.com

Library of Congress Cataloging-in-Publication Data
Knauer, Ian.
   The farm : rustic recipes for a year of incredible food / Ian Knauer ;
photographs by Hirsheimer & Hamilton.
       p. cm.
   Includes index.
   ISBN 978-0-547-51691-2
   1. Cooking, American. 2. Seasonal cooking—United States.
3. Knauer, Ian—Homes and haunts—Pennsylvania—Knauertown.
4. Farm life—Pennsylvania—Knauertown. I. Title.
TX715.K687 2012   641.5973—dc23

Book design by Hirsheimer & Hamilton

Printed in the United States of America
DOW 10 9 8 7 6 5 4 3 2 1

For Daniel Knauer,

who taught me how to work hard and love even harder

❀ ❀ ❀

Acknowledgments

I owe unfathomable thanks to an uncountable number of people for their inspiration, guidance, and help with this book. My parents and sisters are pillars of support and are always the first to volunteer for the most difficult and least rewarding tasks. They never expect thanks, and for that I am most grateful. My aunts and uncles have given me the freedom to make decisions when it comes to the farm. Thank you all: Janet, Larry, Joan, Phil, Ronald, Charlotte, Diane, Joel, Lowell, Denise, Carol, and Doug. A special thanks to Lowell and Denise for their love of all things edible. My cousins are some of my closest friends, and I am convinced that the sweat they pour into the place helps the vegetables grow. Thanks to Leif, Megan, Ryan, Beth, Tim, Adrienne, and Dietrich; without your help, nothing would be worth the effort.

I owe unspeakable gratitude to Ruth Reichl and Doc Willoughby. You have both always been my most vocal cheerleaders.

I have learned more than I realize from the cooks who have taught me. Zanne Stewart, Kemp Minifie, Alexis Touchet, Ruth Cousineau, Paul Grimes, Maggie Ruggiero, Gina Miraglia, Melissa Roberts, Andrea Albin, Kay Chun, and Shelley Wiseman are some of the best I've ever met. Thank you for your guidance. Also, thanks to both Peter Berley and Larry Ingram, who saw promise in me. Thank you all for teaching me to focus on what really matters: the food.

Friends like mine might as well be family. Alan Sytsma, my compatriot in food, is and will always be the most fun addition at any table. Michelli, thank you for support and for keeping me grounded. Rebecca Flaste Karson weeded through flea markets for perfectly imperfect props. Matt Laubner, Jackson Eaton, John Opladen, and Marko Remmel—our friendships are irreplaceable, as you well know; thank you for eating everything I've ever put in front of you. Gerry Campbell, thank you for everything you have given me; chapter three of our lives will be the best yet.

Doe Coover is quite possibly the world's best cookbook agent, and her ability to focus thousands of thoughts into one razor-sharp pitch is a true gift. Rux Martin has taken my story and recipes and molded them into exactly what they should be. Barry Estabrook, thank you for your silent support. I might be your biggest fan.

Christopher Hirsheimer and Melissa Hamilton have sacrificed a large chunk of their summer and have brought the farm to life with their incredible photographs. They are both great teachers and students of food and life. Becoming their friend has been my sincerest pleasure.

Contents

Foreword

IAN FOUND A MARAUDING WOODCHUCK foraging on his farm, and he's turned him into pâté. You have to come taste it; it's pretty great."

Zanne Stewart was standing in the doorway of my office at *Gourmet*, giving me a significant look. I knew exactly what that portended: our executive food editor had something on her mind, and it wasn't just Ian's exotic take on pâté.

Zanne ran the magazine's test kitchen, an almost unimaginably intimidating place. It was divided into eight small fiefdoms, each the domain of an extremely talented—and competitive—cook. Each food editor (*Gourmet*-speak for cook/recipe developer) was an expert in a different field. Paul had lived in France, where he worked for years with Julia Child's collaborator Simca Beck. Ruth, who had once run her own restaurant in Vermont, was deeply admired by Eric Ripert. Gina was the most imaginative baker I've ever encountered, and Maggie had worked her way through New York's finest kitchens—and that is just for starters. We had experts in Chinese, Mexican, Italian, and Korean cooking. Ian, on the other hand, had arrived as a lowly cross-tester: his job was to stand in for the readers and road test every recipe just before it was printed in the magazine. The food editors considered a cross-tester to be a mere amateur. They liked him fine, but he was definitely not one of them.

For four years, Ian held his tongue and held his own, as he quietly tested the food editors' creations. Even when he thought the time had come to demonstrate his expertise, he moved slowly. One spring he came in with honey from his own hives, an elixir of such character that editors stood in line to get their share. Later he came bearing dandelion wine he'd made himself and ramps he'd foraged in the woods. During hunting season that fall, he arrived with the leg of a deer he'd shot, treating us to his version of venison.

The change was subtle, but as the farm-to-table movement gathered momentum, it became clear that Ian had much to teach us. His knowledge was undeniable—and it had become valuable. So when Zanne gave me that look, I knew exactly what she was thinking: it was time for Ian to stop testing everyone else's recipes and start creating some of his own. *Gourmet* needed him.

I probably should have called Ian into my office to deliver the news, but a few minutes later, I passed him on the stairs, and I couldn't keep it to myself. "Ian," I blurted out, "we're promoting you to food editor."

He stared at me for a long moment.

"Shut up!" he said excitedly.

Looking back, I see that it wasn't just our attitude toward Ian that had changed; Ian had changed, too. While he'd been cross-testing all those dishes, transforming himself from a passionate amateur into a real professional, he'd rediscovered his reverence for ingredients—and not just those he grew himself. It was Ian who found the halal slaughterhouse in Brooklyn, insisting that he had to spend the day there. He wanted to pick out his own goat, witness the kill, and then create enough recipes to use up every single morsel of that animal. The story that he and Alan Sytsma wrote was beautiful in many ways, for it truly makes you understand that when you eat a piece of meat, you are consuming life itself. Still, it takes a brave man to carry a warm goat carcass into the Condé Nast building, and an even braver one to waltz into an elevator occupied by *Vogue*'s editor in chief Anna Wintour. All I can say is: I wish I'd been there.

Watching Ian grow as a cook has been truly exciting, but what has been even more thrilling has been watching his food philosophy mature. For him, the farm-to-table mantra isn't a trend or a fad, and it's not something he's ever likely to walk away from. Ian's cooking begins in the garden and the fields; he demands an intimate relationship with his ingredients. Tasting that woodchuck pâté he made, I understood that it was the end of a battle; the woodchuck was gobbling up Ian's hard-won produce. But he was a free-range woodchuck, and he did not die in vain. The pâté was truly delicious.

Reading Ian's book, I am reminded of one of the great (and sadly overlooked) American food writers. Seventy years ago, Angelo Pellegrini had a vision of what a true American food movement might be. A professor of literature at the University of Washington, he was a man who believed so fervently in growing his own food that he ripped out his lawn to plant a garden. He made his own wine, hunted his own meat, and fed his Seattle family on food that he had raised himself. In a time when "American cuisine" was considered a non sequitur, he believed, passionately, that Americans could eat the world's best food if only we would pursue what he called "a life rooted in the earth."

But Pellegrini was searching for more than mere flavor: he believed that the good life is one that you make with your own two hands. He had nothing but contempt for those who hire others to do their gardening and their cooking, for he felt that they were cheating themselves out of the best part of being alive. Reading his words changed my attitude about food.

I feel much the same about this book of Ian's. Most cookbooks are about the end product, about making good food to put on your table. But a great cookbook offers you more than that—it helps you appreciate the process. Ian's recipes will certainly feed you well, but more than that, they will encourage you to savor every moment in the kitchen.

— Ruth Reichl

The Recipes by Category

✳

continued

preserves

desserts

miscellaneous

Introduction

IN A SMALL GRAVEYARD, just off a narrow, winding rural route in Pennsylvania, a head-stone etched entirely in German marks the plot of Johann Christopher Knauer, who died in 1769. He and his family came to their new land to start fresh and named the village Knauertown. I've spent most of my weekends at what is still called the Knauer farm: it has become the only place I really consider home.

The driveway snakes in from the road, past the pond with a rickety dock that wobbles and creaks under the slightest weight, and up the hill toward the house. Somewhere around the gate, I let the dog out of the car. He runs and rolls through the tall grass as I slowly navigate the sharp turns to make my way to the farmhouse. The driveway takes several minutes to travel and is completely transporting. It feels very distinctly like going back in time. The white stucco house, well over a century old, overlooks the pond. Behind the house, fields of waving green grass stretch up the hill until they are met by the tree line. As I step out of the car, I notice how clean the air feels in my lungs. I breathe it in slowly, letting its freshness soak through me. When I am at the farm, I feel as if I am miles—and centuries—away from the rest of the world.

WHEN I WAS in my teens, I hated coming here. Mowing the four-acre lawn was not how I wanted to spend my Saturdays. Neither was chopping cords upon cords of firewood, or helping my father repair the century-old barn's slate roof, or whitewashing the old chicken coop, pigpen, or outhouse—or helping my grandfather with his garden. Now those moments are all I need to be happy. I've come to realize that I am only a small link in the history of the farm that my family has considered home for many, many generations. It's a rare opportunity, and I am lucky to have it. My grandfather felt the same way.

I can't remember a moment when he wasn't at the farm. He was stoic and gruff and, even as an old man, seemed larger than life. But he had a tender side, and more than anything else, he enjoyed spending his time at the farm with his family. I remember when I was a very young boy, walking up the hill with him to his garden, where we picked strawberries. His enormous hand seemed to swallow mine as he lifted me by one arm over the garden fence and landed me gently onto the dirt, my feet surrounded by the bright red berries of early summer. He was loving, gentle, and strong with all his grandchildren. I am the eldest of twenty-four cousins.

Every summer he would grow his strawberries, along with corn, cantaloupe, and so much more. There were more vegetables than we could ever eat. There was more work to do than we could ever finish. And many days he would call me or my sisters in from a sun-scorched field for a break.

My sister Cecily remembers one afternoon in August when our father dropped her off to mow the lawn. Our grandfather told her it was too hot, and she'd have to spend the afternoon sitting on the porch swing instead, chatting with him. She sat next to him, her legs dangling in her cutoff jeans and T-shirt. He wore, as he always did, long khaki work pants and a tucked-in, long-sleeved white shirt. They sat and swung, sometimes in conversation, sometimes in silence, for hours. Later that day, when my father asked Cecily in a scolding tone why the grass was still tall, our grandfather scolded him in turn. He said the work would always be there. What he meant was that he would not. He was right on both counts.

A lot changed during my third decade with the farm. The fields stood unplowed and uncultivated. No one could figure out how to fill the emptiness. The house and the barn felt hollow. Cousins and siblings moved away for college or work, and the farm waited. But change that feels a long time coming can happen in an instant. I recall the instant it happened for me.

One spring, one of our aunts asked for my help planting a few fruit trees. I remember noticing a familiar warmth in the late April morning breeze as I dug holes in the field for those young trees. Near the ancient apple trees, we planted a dwarf apple, an Asian pear, a Hosui pear, and even a fig tree. As we placed the fruit trees in the ground, I could feel a sudden change in the way I felt about the farm. It's a reciprocal sort of place that gives back to me what I've given to it, and tamping cool earth around the trees' roots seemed to usher in a brand-new era. It's one in which I have grown closer to the family, the place, the garden, and the beautiful yet sometimes difficult lessons they have to teach me.

THE HISTORY of the farm can be felt at every turn and every corner. Function and purpose have been the forces behind over a hundred years of landscape decisions, and each generation has added its thumbprint to the face of the property. My father and his siblings have worked hard to preserve the outer edge of the woods, negotiating with preservation groups to enable the natural forest to live on. Our grandfather planted rows of yews, three hundred yards long and twenty feet wide, that provide shelter and a haven for deer. He repaved the driveway to avoid the natural streams and dug out the low wetlands to create a spring-fed pond. He planted many trees. He poured himself into improving this place without encroaching on its history.

Thousands of rocks piled on top of thousands more line the fields of the farm. They work to keep the trees in the woods. They've been working at it ever since they were piled there by hand, the backbreaking labor of our ancestors who cleared these fields. They built the barn

with rocks from the field, and the farmhouse, and the foundations of the old chicken coop, the pigpen, and the wagon shed. Then, with the thousands and thousands of rocks still left, they built the wall. Now, in the fields, there are no rocks to be found. Rockless fields are perfect for gardens, like the one my sisters and I decided to plant this spring.

When our grandfather had grown too old to garden, the fields were not used to farm anything except the hay that we gave to a local farmer in exchange for his cutting it. Our grandfather favored beets, wheat, and potatoes. I remember watching him tow a small plow through the potato plants when I was still too young to help, the creamy white spuds spilling out of the ground, tumbling into the sunlight. My first potato crop was his last.

I called Cecily on the phone early one January morning to propose planting a garden together. Before I could complete the thought, she started to tell me her memories of our grandfather's garden. She told me she'd been searching, in vain, for cherry tomatoes that could live up to her memory of her childhood, when she would stand next to the plants for hours and strip them of their fruits, popping each little tomato into her mouth, one at a time. We decided to give the garden a try.

The prospect of a summer brimming with fresh vegetables of every variety may have gotten us a little too excited. Instead of starting with a reasonable number of tomato plants for three small families, my sisters and I grew sixty, of which fifty-six made it through the season. We had so many tomatoes that we couldn't give them away. After eating them raw off the plants, in every meal for a month, canning, freezing, and dehydrating them, we still could have built a wall of tomatoes comparable, it seemed, to the wall of rocks that lined the fields.

We planted too much zucchini, too. And too much fennel, hot chile peppers (Scotch bonnet, fatali, malagueta, chocolate habanero, peach habanero, and poblano), okra, Brussels sprouts, carrots, parsley (flat-leaf and root), corn (sweet and hominy), beans (French and green), radishes, arugula, lettuce, beets (pronto and salad leaf), chard (red and orange), scallions, onions, garlic, cucumbers (burpless and Kirby), butternut squash, and potatoes (Red Bliss and purple).

Oh, and then there were the herbs. By sometime in mid-July, we were swimming in oceans of dill, cilantro (slow-bolt, regular, and Vietnamese), basil (lime, regular, and purple), thyme, oregano, mint, rosemary, and lavender.

We wondered what to do with it all: our eyes were bigger than our refrigerators. But when life hands you fifty-six tomato plants, there's only one thing to do: make lots and lots of sauce.

THIS BOOK IS a journal of abundance and the beginning of a new generation's thumbprint on what has become an ancient family tradition. Chapters follow the seasons of the garden, beginning in the early spring and ending well into the winter.

Most of these recipes are quick and easy to prepare, making them especially attractive to those of us who need to balance dinnertime with work. They get the best food to the table in the least amount of time. They are geared toward the American palate, which has become increasingly sophisticated in recent years, incorporating flavors from Italy and France alongside those from Mexico and Asia. In the end, this book offers recipes for every kind of cook, from the most basic to the most experienced.

The recipes highlight vegetables at their peak, following the subtle changes in the garden. They are flavorful, modern takes on American classics, with accessible ingredients that anyone can procure, such as bacon, olive oil, and garlic.

One chapter is devoted to larger projects for kitchen gardeners and more ambitious cooks. Basic preservation methods, such as making chile-infused vinegar and quick radish pickles in the spring, lead to canning tomatoes and pickling cucumbers in the summer, then to making pumpkin puree and fermenting cider in the fall. Many of these methods have been passed down to me from my grandparents.

Whether you are an overachieving amateur farmer like me or an overexcited produce patron, these simple recipes will, I hope, become standards at your dinner table, as they have at mine.

Spring Planting

MY SISTERS, Cecily and Haley, and I had been impatiently waiting for this moment. We stood side by side, our bare feet sinking into the spring rain–soaked and freshly plowed soil that would soon become our garden. The air, especially humid for early May, smelled sweet and thick and was strangely still.

Each of us had saved seeds from our favorite tomatoes of the past summer. We had started the plants weeks ago. Every square inch of my tiny one-bedroom Brooklyn apartment was covered with planters and grow lamps. From outside on the street, the place glowed neon pink. It's a small miracle that the police didn't come knocking on the door, wondering just what I was growing.

Bringing the plants to the farm was a difficult task. As soon as I had carefully placed them in the backseat of the car, wedging them in so they might not shift, the dog decided the little eggplant seedlings looked as comfortable as a bed and lay down on top of them.

We had convinced the neighboring farmer, who collected the hay from our fields, to plow us a football-field-sized plot, small by his standards. On the phone, he told us that farming was different now. His own field, where he grew corn, hadn't been plowed in almost ten years, just mowed with a huge tractor, injected with chemicals, and reseeded every spring.

But we were going to do things the hard way. First, though, we had to break up the clumps of sod that the farmer had plowed under with his tractor.

It turns out that 1952 was a good year to buy a tractor from the Ford Motor Company. Ours, rickety looking but hardy, started up immediately and ran through the spring soil, pulling the ancient disks behind it, making easy work of the clumps. In less than an hour, we were ready to plant. Haley invited along a handful of city friends, and we grabbed the seed packages from a pile and started work.

Planting vegetable seeds is an inspiring way to spend a morning. Every seed placed in a row or patch is a forward-looking hope.

We set up twine in straight lines every few feet and pushed the soil to the side with hand tools. Every few inches, we pressed seeds into the damp ground then covered them back up again. It felt good to get that chore done, but the freshly seeded garden looked barren. We stood there, sucking down well-deserved beers and staring at a huge mud patch.

Within five days, tiny arugula sprouts had popped up in a single file, reaching for the sun. I bent down and pulled one from its rank, placing it in my mouth. It exploded with pepper, and I felt the heat from the leaves radiating through my smile.

That first week, something burrowed a five-inch-diameter tunnel under the far corner of the garden's fence. It seemed as though nothing was missing from the garden, so I didn't give it further thought. I filled the hole in with rocks and went inside to cook a roast chicken for everyone.

Artichokes with Souped-Up Mayo serves 4

This recipe is one of the secret weapons of any dinner. Artichokes, which usually require at least 45 minutes to steam, take only 10 to 12 minutes when you use a pressure cooker (one of my favorite kitchen tools). Add some lemon and smoked paprika to regular mayo, and you've got a near-perfect dipping sauce. Let your guests peel the leaves away as they chat over cocktails, and supply a spoon so they can dig out the choke before eating the heart, dipped, of course, in the mayo.

4 artichokes

½ cup water

½ cup mayonnaise

1 teaspoon finely grated lemon zest

2 teaspoons lemon juice

½ teaspoon smoked paprika

¼ teaspoon kosher salt

¼ teaspoon black pepper

Trim the bottom ¼ inch off the artichoke stems. Peel the outer layer of each stem. Place the artichokes in a pressure cooker with the water. Seal the lid and bring the pressure cooker up to high pressure. Cook at high pressure until the artichokes are very tender and can be easily pierced with a sharp knife, 10 to 12 minutes.

Stir together the mayonnaise, lemon zest, juice, paprika, salt, and pepper.

Serve the artichokes warm or at room temperature with the souped-up mayonnaise.

Soft-Boiled Eggs with Watercress and Walnut-Ricotta Crostini serves 4

For generations American farm women would cook a simple meal of toast, eggs, farmer cheese, and whatever they could gather from the woods, like watercress and walnuts. This recipe weaves those familiar elements into a dish you might find at any higher-end city restaurant. There's something simple and sexy about a soft-cooked egg: it instantly elevates any dish. Here, peppery watercress and light lemon dressing counter the rich yolk. This dish makes for an impressive breakfast or first course or a satisfying lunch.

3 tablespoons unsalted butter

4 slices sourdough bread

½ cup walnut pieces

½ cup fresh ricotta (see page 22)

2 tablespoons lemon juice

Kosher salt and black pepper

4 large eggs

2 cups watercress

Extra-virgin olive oil or walnut oil for drizzling (optional)

Heat 2 tablespoons of the butter in a large heavy skillet over medium heat until it melts. Add the bread slices to the skillet and toast until both sides are well browned, 3 to 4 minutes. Remove the bread and add the remaining 1 tablespoon butter to the skillet, along with the walnuts. Toast the walnuts, stirring them occasionally, until they are lightly browned, about 3 minutes. Transfer the walnuts, along with any butter in the skillet, to a food processor. Let the walnuts cool completely, then add the ricotta, 1 tablespoon of the lemon juice, and ½ teaspoon each salt and pepper and pulse until well combined.

Place the eggs in a small saucepan and cover with room-temperature water (hot water on cold eggs causes the shells to crack). Bring the water to a boil, turn off the heat, cover the saucepan, and let stand for 2 minutes. (For yolks that are cooked through, leave the eggs in the hot water for 10 minutes.) Remove the eggs and place them under cold running water for about 30 seconds. Peel the eggs under cold running water.

Toss the watercress with the remaining 1 tablespoon lemon juice, ½ teaspoon salt, and ¼ teaspoon pepper.

Spread the walnut ricotta evenly over the toasts, then top with the watercress. Place 1 egg over each crostini and season to taste with salt and pepper. Gently cut the egg open to break the yolk, letting it run down to dress the watercress. Drizzle with oil, if desired, and serve.

Cheese Grits Nuggets serves 4 to 6

If I walked into a bar that served these tasty nuggets as snacks, I might never leave. Luckily for my wallet, these little puppies (they're similar to hush puppies but creamier and more intense) are easy and cheap to make at home. The idea for this appetizer/side dish/snack came from a Brooklyn restaurant called Peaches HotHouse, which specializes in Southern food. There the "grits fries" are served alongside fried chicken. I've added a lot of cheese to make them into a decadent yet homey finger food. Serve them for breakfast or dinner, with cocktails, or when you're watching the game. These nuggets are great on their own but are even better when dipped in Souped-Up Mayo (page 4).

3 cups water

¾ cup grits

1 teaspoon kosher salt

½ teaspoon black pepper

4 ounces cheddar cheese,
    cut into ¼-inch pieces

3 cups vegetable oil for frying

½ cup fine cornmeal

1 tablespoon chili powder

Lightly oil an 8-inch square baking dish.

Bring the water to a boil in a heavy medium saucepan. Whisk in the grits, ½ teaspoon of the salt, and ¼ teaspoon of the pepper. Simmer the grits, whisking frequently, until they are tender, 15 to 20 minutes. Stir in the cheese and pour into the baking dish. Cover the surface with a layer of lightly oiled waxed paper, then cool completely in the refrigerator for at least 4 hours.

Heat the oil in a heavy medium saucepan to 425°F.

Cut the grits into 32 rectangles (about 1 by 3 inches). Stir together the cornmeal, chili powder, the remaining ½ teaspoon salt, and the remaining ¼ teaspoon pepper. Roll the rectangles in the cornmeal mixture, then fry them in batches, turning, and reheating the oil to 425°F before frying the next batch, until golden, about 4 minutes per batch. Transfer the nuggets to paper towels to cool slightly, and serve.

Spaghetti with Arugula Carbonara serves 4 to 6

No matter the time of year, I can always count on a few constants in the kitchen: bacon, eggs, dried pasta, onions, garlic, olive oil, and cheese. Because the ingredients for this classic Italian pasta dish are usually on hand, carbonara should be in every cook's repertoire. It's a perfect dinner to make when you have only a handful of staples and no time (or willpower) to truck to the store to buy more food. Peppery arugula adds great freshness.

6 slices bacon, chopped

2 tablespoons extra-virgin
    olive oil

1 large onion, thinly sliced

3 garlic cloves, thinly sliced

Kosher salt and black pepper

12 ounces spaghetti

2 large eggs

¼ cup finely grated Parmigiano-
    Reggiano

5 ounces baby arugula

Cook the bacon, oil, onion, garlic, ½ teaspoon salt, and ¼ teaspoon pepper in a large heavy skillet over medium heat until the onion is golden, about 10 minutes.

Cook the pasta in a large pot of heavily salted boiling water until it is al dente. Meanwhile, whisk together the eggs, Parmesan, and ¼ teaspoon each salt and pepper in a large bowl. Reserve 1 cup of the pasta-cooking water, then drain the pasta.

Toss the pasta with the egg mixture, onion mixture, arugula, and ½ cup of the pasta-cooking water until the greens are wilted. Thin the sauce with additional pasta-cooking water, if desired. Season to taste with salt and pepper and serve immediately.

Wheat Beer Chicken   serves 4

This recipe takes its flavors from one of the classic European beers: Belgian *witbier*. This style, which often includes orange peel and coriander seeds in the process, leads to unexpectedly wonderful flavors in the final brew — flavors that also happen to pair well with roast chicken. So does beer.

1 (3½-pound) chicken

2 tablespoons unsalted butter, at room temperature

1 teaspoon finely grated orange zest

½ teaspoon ground coriander

2 teaspoons kosher salt

½ teaspoon black pepper

1 large garlic clove, smashed

½ orange, cut in half

1 cup wheat beer, such as Blue Moon, hefeweizen, or Shock Top

1 teaspoon cornstarch

1 tablespoon water

Preheat the oven to 450°F, with a rack in the middle.

Rinse the chicken and pat it dry. Work together the butter, orange zest, coriander, and ½ teaspoon of the salt. Working your way back from the large cavity, gently run your fingers between the chicken skin and the meat to loosen the skin, being careful not to tear it. Push the butter under the skin, including the thighs and drumsticks, and massage the skin from the outside to spread the butter evenly. Season the chicken inside and out with the remaining 1½ teaspoons salt and the pepper. Put the garlic and orange in the cavity and loosely tie the legs together with kitchen string.

Roast the chicken in a flameproof roasting pan, liberally basting with some of the beer every 15 minutes, until it is golden and the skin pulls away from the base of the drumsticks, about 50 minutes. Transfer the chicken to a cutting board and let it rest for 15 minutes before carving.

Set the roasting pan over a burner and add the remaining beer. Bring the liquid to a simmer, scraping up any browned bits. Stir together the cornstarch and water, then stir the mixture into the simmering pan juices. Simmer the gravy, stirring, until it is slightly thickened, about 1 minute. Strain the gravy, if desired, and serve with the chicken.

Cast-Iron-Seared Cornish Hens
with Baby Potatoes and Chives serves 4

Cast-iron pans are the original nonstick skillets, and they add flavor through their ability to sear and the seasoning they've acquired from age. The potatoes that roast alongside these birds soak up the juices and are infused with flavor.

There's another secret ingredient here: La Quercia Speck Americano — which, despite its exotic name, is actually made in Norwalk, Iowa. Similar to prosciutto, speck, which originated on the Italian-Austrian border, is a cured pork leg that has been smoked at a low heat until it becomes beautifully pink. Best served very thinly sliced, it differs from prosciutto in its spices, which are heavy on juniper and garlic, and in its smokiness. Speck adds a whole new level of salty, fatty flavor, so track some down if you can (you can buy it online at www.laquercia.us). Otherwise, prosciutto makes a worthy substitute.

2 Cornish hens (about 2 pounds each)

1 lemon, thinly sliced crosswise

1 small shallot, thinly sliced

3 tablespoons extra-virgin olive oil

1½ teaspoons kosher salt

¾ teaspoon black pepper

2 pounds baby potatoes, halved or quartered if large

4 ounces thinly sliced speck (see headnote) or prosciutto

¼ cup chopped fresh chives

Preheat the oven to 450°F, with a rack in the middle.

Rinse the hens and pat dry. Remove the backbones by cutting along each side of them with a pair of kitchen shears, then place the birds on a work surface, skin side up. Press down with the palm of your hand to crack the breastbone and flatten.

Toss the lemon, shallot, 2 tablespoons of the oil, the salt, and pepper in a large bowl. Toss the hens in the marinade and marinate at room temperature for 45 minutes to 1 hour. Lift the hens out of the marinade, reserving the lemon slices and the marinade in the bowl.

Heat the remaining 1 tablespoon oil in a large cast-iron skillet over medium-high heat until it shimmers. Brown the hens, skin side down, for about 7 minutes total. Transfer the hens to a plate, then add the potatoes and the marinade (and the lemon slices) to the skillet. Place the hens on top of the potatoes skin side up, along with any juices from the plate, and transfer the skillet to the oven. Roast until the hens are cooked through, 20 to 25 minutes. Transfer the hens to a serving plate and let them stand for 10 minutes. Meanwhile, return the skillet with the potatoes to the oven to finish cooking, 5 to 10 minutes.

When the potatoes are tender, transfer them to the serving plate with the hens, scattering them around the birds. Tear the speck and drape it over and around the potatoes. Sprinkle the chives over the potatoes and serve.

Paprika Pork Chops
with Scallion-Citrus Relish serves 4

This scallion-citrus relish uses flavors that echo Asian cuisine and accompanies a pork chop that uses Spanish smoked paprika. The recipe comes with an important lesson attached: don't overlook scallions. Give them a little love, and they become incredible. In this bright, easy-to-make sauce, the citrus tempers their sharpness.

1 bunch scallions (about 8 ounces)

2 lemons

1 orange

1 teaspoon sugar

3 tablespoons extra-virgin olive oil

2 teaspoons kosher salt

1¼ teaspoons black pepper

4 (1-inch-thick) bone-in center-cut pork chops

1½ teaspoons smoked paprika

¾ teaspoon ground coriander

Slice the scallions very thinly on a long diagonal. Grate 1 teaspoon zest from the lemons and 1 teaspoon zest from the orange. With a sharp paring knife, cut away the peel from the lemons and orange, slicing down around the fruit, removing all the white pith. Working over a bowl, cut the segments free from the membranes, letting the segments fall into the bowl. Remove the segments and chop, reserving any juice in the bowl. Add the chopped citrus, scallions, zests, sugar, 2 tablespoons of the oil, ¾ teaspoon of the salt, and ½ teaspoon of the pepper to the juice in the bowl, stirring to combine the relish.

Rinse the pork chops and pat dry. Stir together the paprika, coriander, the remaining 1¼ teaspoons salt, and the remaining ¾ teaspoon pepper, then rub the spice mixture onto both sides of the chops.

Heat the remaining 1 tablespoon oil in a large heavy skillet over medium heat until it shimmers. Cook the pork chops, in batches if necessary, turning once, until golden and slightly pink in the center, 8 to 10 minutes total.

Transfer the pork chops to plates and let stand for 10 minutes. Serve the pork chops with the relish.

Dried-Fruit-Braised Short Ribs serves 4

I'd grown bored with the same old red-wine-and-beef-stock braising liquid, so one cold spring night, I decided to take another route. Short ribs have serious flavor and heft, so I added dried fruits and spices that are usually associated with stronger meats, like lamb.

   The result is a perfect sweet-and-sour balance to the fatty, decadent meat. After hours of cooking, the fruit melts into the braising liquid and the meat starts to fall off the bone. For a satisfying, warming meal, pair with Twice-Baked Chipotle Potatoes (page 19) and Molasses-Orange-Glazed Carrots (page 16).

4 bone-in beef short ribs (about 2 pounds total)

Kosher salt and black pepper

2 tablespoons extra-virgin olive oil or Master Fat (page 23)

3 large shallots, sliced

3 garlic cloves, thinly sliced

2 cups water

1 cup dried apricots

1 cup pitted prunes

¼ cup light or dark brown sugar

1 tablespoon apple cider vinegar

½ teaspoon ground cinnamon

¼ teaspoon ground allspice

¼ teaspoon ground cloves

1 tablespoon all-purpose flour

Preheat the oven to 350°F.

Pat the beef dry, then season it with 1½ teaspoons salt and 1 teaspoon pepper. Heat the oil in a large heavy ovenproof pot over high heat until it shimmers. Brown the ribs on both sides, about 8 minutes total. Transfer the ribs to a plate. Pour off all but 2 tablespoons fat from the pot (add it to your Master Fat), add the shallots and garlic, and cook, stirring occasionally, until they are browned, 5 to 7 minutes. Add the ribs and any juices on the plate back to the pot along with the water, apricots, prunes, brown sugar, vinegar, and spices, stirring to combine. Cover the pot with a tight-fitting lid and transfer it to the oven. Braise until the ribs are falling off the bone, 3½ to 4 hours.

Remove the short ribs from the braising liquid and pour the braising liquid through a sieve, reserving the fruit. Skim off the fat from the braising liquid, reserving 1 tablespoon of the fat. Return the braising liquid to the pot, along with the dried fruit. Bring the liquid to a simmer over medium-high heat. Stir together the reserved 1 tablespoon fat and the flour, then whisk the mixture into the simmering liquid. Cook until the sauce is slightly thickened, about 8 minutes. Season the sauce with salt and pepper to taste. Serve the short ribs with the sauce.

Spring Pork Stew serves 6 to 8

Navarin d'agneau, a traditional French lamb stew featuring spring's first vegetables, is the inspiration for this warming stew. I use pork instead of lamb, and the broth from simmering the pork is a deeply flavored foundation for bright, fresh veggies pulled straight from the garden. I add a finishing touch of rich cream, inspired by *blanquette de veau,* a white veal stew. The result is an all-new stew, the ideal dinner for those not-quite-warm-enough spring nights.

1 celery stalk

1 carrot

1 shallot

4 garlic cloves

1 (3½-pound) bone-in pork butt (shoulder)

Kosher salt and black pepper

2 tablespoons extra-virgin olive oil or Master Fat (page 23)

1 cup dry white wine

4 cups chicken stock or low-sodium broth

1 bay leaf

1 thyme sprig

8 ounces baby carrots

8 ounces baby zucchini (about 3 inches long), halved

8 ounces baby turnips, quartered

1 cup heavy cream

Pulse the celery, carrot, shallot, and garlic in a food processor until finely chopped or finely chop by hand.

Rub the pork with 1¼ teaspoons salt and ½ teaspoon pepper. Heat the oil in a heavy pot over medium-high heat until it shimmers. Brown the pork on all sides, 8 to 12 minutes. Transfer the pork to a plate.

Pour off all but 2 tablespoons fat from the pan (add it to your Master Fat), add the finely chopped vegetables, and cook, stirring occasionally, until they are browned, about 6 minutes. Add the wine to the pot, bring to a simmer, and cook until it is reduced by half, about 2 minutes. Add the chicken stock, the pork with any juices from the plate, and the bay leaf and thyme (the liquid may not completely cover the pork and that's OK). Reduce the heat to low, so the liquid is barely simmering, and cover the pot. Simmer the stew until the pork is falling off the bone, about 4 hours. Discard the bay leaf and skim the fat from the surface.

Transfer the pork to a work surface. Discard the bone and any tough bits, then coarsely shred the meat and return it to the pot. Bring the stew back to a boil and add the baby carrots. Simmer the carrots for 5 minutes, add the zucchini and turnips, and continue simmering until the vegetables are tender, 6 to 8 minutes more. Stir in the cream and bring the stew back to a simmer. If a thicker consistency is desired, continue to simmer the stew until it is slightly thickened. Season with salt and pepper to taste and serve in bowls.

Chicken Stew with
Dill-Scallion Dumplings serves 6 to 8

All too often, dumplings taste more like little flour bricks than comforting clouds of dough. If you're used to those versions, you might be hesitant to try this stew, but after just one bite, you'll agree that these dumplings are mind-changing. If you have leftovers, store the stew and the dumplings in separate containers in the fridge. When you reheat them, place the dumplings on top of the cold stew and cover the pot to keep the dumplings from getting too solid.

For the stew

2 tablespoons Master Fat (page 23) or extra-virgin olive oil

1 large onion, chopped

2 carrots, chopped

2 parsnips, chopped

1 celery stalk, chopped

3 garlic cloves, finely chopped

Kosher salt and black pepper

1 (3½-pound) chicken

2 bay leaves

8 cups water

For the dumplings

2 cups all-purpose flour

4 teaspoons baking powder

3 tablespoons unsalted butter, cut into tablespoon-sized pieces

1 teaspoon kosher salt

¼ teaspoon black pepper

2 tablespoons finely chopped scallion greens (reserve the whites for the mustard cream)

2 tablespoons finely chopped fresh dill

¾ cup whole milk

Make the stew: Heat the fat in a heavy medium pot over medium-high heat until it is hot. Stir in the onion, carrots, parsnips, celery, garlic, 1½ teaspoons salt, and ½ teaspoon pepper. Cook, stirring occasionally, until the vegetables start to brown, 6 to 8 minutes. Add the chicken, bay leaves, and water (the water may not completely cover the chicken and that's OK). Bring the water to a simmer, then cover the pot. Reduce the heat to medium-low and simmer the stew until the chicken is very tender, about 1½ hours. Discard the bay leaves. Remove the chicken from the pot and let it cool slightly. Remove the meat from the chicken and cut it into bite-sized pieces. Discard the bones and skin. Return the meat to the pot and season the stew with salt and pepper to taste.

Make the dumplings: Work together the flour, baking powder, butter, salt, and pepper with your hands until mostly combined, with some small lumps of butter remaining. Stir in the scallion greens and dill. Stir in the milk with a fork until the dough just comes together.

Bring the stew to a simmer, then drop heaping tablespoons of the dumpling dough over the stew. Cover the pot and cook until the dumplings are puffed and appear dry on the surface, 15 to 20 minutes.

For the mustard cream

2 tablespoons finely chopped
scallion whites

2 tablespoons finely chopped
fresh dill

1 tablespoon Dijon mustard

¼ cup heavy cream

Kosher salt and black pepper

Make the mustard cream: Stir together the scallion whites, dill, and mustard. Beat the cream until it holds soft peaks, then fold in the mustard mixture. Season with salt and pepper to taste.

Serve the chicken stew and dumplings in bowls, topped with the mustard cream.

Baby Lettuce Salad with Avocado Dressing   serves 6 as a first course

All you need is a spoon and a pinch of salt for an avocado to be an unctuous snack. Here, avocado lends its smooth, fatty texture to the dressing, making it supercreamy without a lot of oil. It also adds a mellow, green flavor that coats the baby lettuce, which has a more intense flavor than older lettuce.

½ very ripe avocado, pitted

1 tablespoon extra-virgin
olive oil

1 tablespoon lime juice

½ tablespoon finely chopped
shallot

¼ teaspoon sugar

1 teaspoon kosher salt

½ teaspoon black pepper

8 ounces mixed baby greens,
such as kale, mizuna, tatsoi,
mustard, arugula, and spinach
(16 cups)

Puree the avocado, oil, lime juice, shallot, sugar, salt, and pepper in a blender. Transfer to a large bowl. Add the greens, toss until coated well, and serve.

Molasses-Orange-Glazed Carrots serves 6

Glazed carrots are the kind of side dish that feels both homey and a little sophisticated. This unusual twist on the classic balances the carrots' natural sweetness with the slight bitter edge of an ever-present country pantry ingredient: molasses. Save the rest of the jar to make Grandma McLean's Molasses Crumb Cupcakes (page 225).

2 medium shallots, sliced

2 tablespoons unsalted butter or Master Fat (page 23)

1½ pounds carrots

1 teaspoon finely grated orange zest

½ cup orange juice

½ cup water

⅓ cup molasses

Kosher salt and black pepper

2 teaspoons fresh thyme leaves

Cook the shallots in the butter in a large heavy skillet over medium-high heat until they are golden brown, 4 to 6 minutes.

Cut the carrots into rounds, then add them to the skillet along with the orange zest, juice, water, molasses, 1¼ teaspoons salt, and ½ teaspoon pepper. Bring the liquid to a boil and cover the skillet with a tight-fitting lid. Cook until the carrots are very tender, about 20 minutes. Uncover and continue to boil until the liquid is reduced to a glaze, about 5 minutes. Stir in the thyme, season with salt and pepper to taste, and serve.

Creamed Spring Onions
with Wine and Bacon serves 6 to 8

Think of this side dish, which has its roots buried deeply in the cuisine of Alsace, as onions carbonara. The smoky, creamy spring onions are right at home with Cast-Iron-Seared Cornish Hens with Baby Potatoes and Chives (page 10) or served over crusty bread for lunch. This is also a great way to use up those beautiful spring onions that you find at your local farmers' market (or in your garden). Once cooked, the onions keep in the fridge for up to a month, but they won't last that long, because you'll want to put them on everything.

2½ pounds spring onions with greens

4 ounces bacon, chopped

1½ teaspoons kosher salt

1 teaspoon black pepper

1 cup dry white wine

¼ cup sour cream

1 teaspoon sugar

½ teaspoon freshly grated nutmeg

Clean the onions, peeling away any dirty outer layers. Cut the bulbs and pale green parts into ½-inch wedges and slice the greens and any flower stalks into ½-inch pieces.

Cook the bacon in a large heavy skillet over medium heat, stirring occasionally, until it is browned, about 8 minutes. Transfer the bacon with a slotted spoon to paper towels, leaving any fat in the skillet. Stir the onions and flower stalks, reserving the greens, into the bacon fat in the pan along with 1 teaspoon of the salt and ½ teaspoon of the pepper. Cook, stirring occasionally, until the onions are browned, 10 to 12 minutes.

Stir in the wine and the onion greens and bring to a simmer. Cook the onions, stirring occasionally, until all of the liquid is evaporated, about 10 minutes.

Remove the skillet from the heat and stir in the sour cream, sugar, nutmeg, and the remaining ½ teaspoon each salt and pepper. Sprinkle the onions with the reserved bacon and serve.

Twice-Baked Chipotle Potatoes serves 4

Let's face it, early spring in the Northeast still feels a whole lot like winter. One thing that can help with making it through the cold is a creamy, smoky twice-baked potato. This one incorporates a newish pantry staple borrowed from Mexican cuisine: chipotles in adobo. Cans of these smoldering chiles are available at almost every grocery store, and once they're opened, they keep in the fridge for months.

4 (8-ounce) russet potatoes

½ cup sour cream

4 ounces grated cheddar cheese

1 tablespoon finely chopped chipotle with some adobo

2 scallions, finely chopped

1 teaspoon dried oregano

1 teaspoon kosher salt

½ teaspoon black pepper

Preheat the oven to 375°F, with a rack in the upper third.

Prick the potatoes a few times with a fork and place on a baking sheet. Bake the potatoes until they are tender, about 1 hour. Let the potatoes cool for about 20 minutes, until cool enough to handle. Increase the oven temperature to 425°F.

Cut off the tops of the potatoes, then scoop the flesh from the tops into a bowl. Scoop out the flesh from the bottoms of the potatoes, leaving about a ¼-inch shell. Mash the potato flesh with the sour cream, cheese, chipotle, scallions, oregano, salt, and pepper. Fill the potato shells with the potato mixture, mounding it on top. Bake the potatoes until the stuffing is hot and browned in places, about 20 minutes. Serve.

Rhubarb–Sour Cream Crostata   serves 6 to 8

A little bit of cornmeal in the crust adds a nutty note to this rustic spring pie. Rhubarb is a favorite of my cousin Leif, who, when he met this pie for the first time at the farm, ate it in slices—wide-eyed and smiling—right from the pie tin, as if it were a dessert pizza.

For the pastry dough

1¼ cups all-purpose flour

¼ cup finely ground cornmeal

1 teaspoon light brown sugar

1 stick unsalted butter, cut into cubes

½ teaspoon kosher salt

2–3 tablespoons cold water

For the filling

¼ cup sour cream

5 cups sliced (1-inch pieces) rhubarb (1 pound)

¾ cup sugar

1 teaspoon finely grated lemon zest

Make the pastry dough: Work together the flour, cornmeal, brown sugar, butter, and salt with your hands until it is mostly combined, with some small lumps of butter remaining. Stir in 2 tablespoons of the water with a fork. Press a small handful of dough together: if it looks powdery and does not come together, stir in the remaining 1 tablespoon water. Transfer the dough to a sheet of plastic wrap. Using the edge of the plastic, fold the dough over on itself, pressing until it comes together. Form the dough into a disk, wrap completely in the plastic, and chill for 1 hour.

Preheat the oven to 425°F, with a rack in the middle.

On a well-floured surface, roll out the pastry dough with a floured rolling pin into a 12-inch round. Place the dough in a 10-inch pie tin.

Make the filling: Spread the sour cream evenly over the bottom of the crust. Toss the rhubarb with the sugar and lemon zest, then spread the fruit evenly over the sour cream. Fold the border of dough up and over the edge of the fruit.

Bake the crostata until the crust is golden, the filling is bubbling, and the rhubarb has started to brown, 45 to 50 minutes. Cool on a rack and serve warm or at room temperature.

Lemon Pudding Cake   serves 6

This two-layer dessert, with its dense, pudding-like bottom and light, fluffy top, is adapted from my grandmother's original recipe — I've reduced the sugar a bit. She served hers warm, topped with whipped cream.

4 large eggs, separated

1 teaspoon finely grated lemon zest

⅓ cup lemon juice

1 tablespoon unsalted butter, melted

1 cup sugar

½ cup all-purpose flour

½ teaspoon kosher salt

1½ cups whole milk

Place a large pan on a rack in the middle of the oven. Fill the pan halfway with water. Preheat the oven to 350°F. Butter an 8-inch square baking dish.

Whisk together the egg yolks, lemon zest, juice, and butter in a large bowl until well combined. Stir together the sugar, flour, and salt, then whisk half of the sugar mixture into the egg-yolk mixture. Whisk in half the milk, then the remaining sugar mixture. Whisk in the remaining milk.

Beat the egg whites to soft peaks, then gently fold them into the batter.

Pour the batter into the baking dish. Place the dish in the pan of water in the oven and bake until the cake is set, about 45 minutes. Cool slightly on a rack. Serve warm or at room temperature.

Buttermilk Ricotta   makes about 1 quart

Fresh ricotta is one of the easiest things to make. In this version, buttermilk's acidity separates the curds from the whey. The resulting fresh cheese has a softer texture and a little more tang than the store-bought kind. Fresh ricotta is great in just about anything, from Soft-Boiled Eggs with Watercress and Walnut-Ricotta Crostini (page 5) to Swiss Chard and Fresh Ricotta Pizza (page 114). Or do as I do and drizzle a bowl of buttermilk ricotta with honey for a simple breakfast or with olive oil and fresh chopped chiles to serve with pita chips at cocktail time.

1 gallon whole milk

3 cups buttermilk

½ cup heavy cream

2 teaspoons kosher salt

Place the milk, buttermilk, cream, and salt in a large pot and slowly bring to a boil, stirring to prevent scorching on the bottom of the pot. Just before the liquid comes to a simmer (it will look very curdled), pour it through a fine-mesh sieve lined with several layers of cheesecloth. Let the cheese drain completely, about 30 minutes. The ricotta keeps, refrigerated and covered, for up to 1 week.

COOKING WITH RENDERED ANIMAL FAT has been embraced around the world for millennia. The Jews and Germans use schmaltz (rendered chicken fat or pork fat, depending on whether they're Jewish or German). The Chinese fry in rendered animal fats. Chicago has become famous for duck-fat French fries. The English have been cooking with beef suet since before medieval times. My grandmother uses bacon fat as the base of the dressing for dandelion greens.

At the hip Brooklyn restaurant Fatty 'Cue, chef Zakary Pelaccio serves an appetizer of toasted fingers of Chinatown white bread and a ramekin of fat rendered from every animal cooked in the kitchen, which he calls "Master Fat." Each fat in the mix brings its own personality. There is smokiness from bacon and heartiness from beef, the quirky funk of lamb and the delicate richness of chicken. Together in the ramekin of warm fat, the separate flavors mingle to become much greater than their parts. There is another advantage to combining the fats in one jar: it's a space-saver.

Anytime you cook bacon for breakfast or sear short ribs for dinner, fat is rendered from the meat. Simply pour or skim it (keeping any browned bits in the pan) into a pint-sized canning jar. Cover the jar with a lid to prevent the fat from absorbing any flavors that might float through your fridge. Every other week or so, place the jar, covered, in a pot of warm water to meld all the flavors together. If your Master Fat has been sitting unused in the fridge for a while, give it a sniff for any off-smelling odors, but as long as the fats are in constant rotation, it will last indefinitely without becoming rancid.

I use Master Fat for almost everything: to sear meats and sauté vegetables or to pan-fry sweet cakes to give them a savory hint. If you cook a lot, I recommend that you keep a jar in your fridge, too. It's a simple way to add deep flavor to anything you cook.

A Single Spear of Asparagus

AT THE FIRST HINT of sun, the sounds of the morning creep in slowly at the farm: the wary skitter of a squirrel in the walnut tree cues a songbird's self-conscious warm-up. Before there is real light, a red fox glides through the faint blue hue of the field. The color of the air changes from blues and greens to pale yellows.

In the early morning of late May, I stood at the edge of the garden and watched the baby radishes stretch their first heart-shaped leaves up and out in full embrace of the sun. Overnight, the pea tendrils had twirled themselves around fence links and southernmost garden posts. A new lilac-colored pea flower swayed under the weight of a honeybee. I followed the bee as she made her way back to the hive.

By midday, trees creaked and swayed, their branches sighing in the breeze. Apple blossoms wafted and fluttered like snowflakes, and a low, deep gray cloud crept ominously from the northwest corner of the sky. The bees, sensitive to the change, increased their hum. The air smelled like copper. Rain came in a hush of sound and a graying of light. I climbed the steps to the front porch of the house, sat on the porch swing, and watched as the rain laid itself onto the surface of the pond.

In half an hour, the rain stopped, and I walked back up to the garden, where next to a young Asian pear tree I found a single spear of asparagus growing in the field. I'd never seen it before, and now it was more than three feet tall, almost ready to flower. I wondered why I hadn't noticed it the day before or the past week, because surely it must have been there.

No one had planted an asparagus crown here for at least thirty years, and this one had to be at least as old as I was. When I dug the hole for the Asian pear six years ago, I would have spaded up the asparagus crown if I'd pushed the shovel in three feet to the west. Knowing little about asparagus care, I wondered if the crown could be encouraged. Was it a signal of hope, a flare? If I cut it off, would the crown send up two or even three more spears next year? Or was this the last attempt of a thirty-year-old crown? I wanted it to live on.

I called my father. He said it must have been my grandfather who put the crown in the field. He guessed he might have eaten from this plant when he was a young man. He told me I should dig it up, split it in half, and replant it in the garden away from the tall grass, where it might find less competition and new vigor.

I dug up the crown: a clump of dirt with thick roots growing from the center. I moved it into the garden and cut it in half, planting the two smaller clumps separately. I watered them. The single spear of asparagus was still attached to one of the pieces and stuck up through the earth. Two weeks later it had flowered and grown long and spindly, and it shimmied when the breeze blew.

Next spring is already planned, and every morning I can, I'll walk to the edge of the garden and look for spears breaking through the thawing ground. I might even buy a new crown and plant it next to the old one as a sort of botanical encouragement and as a way to feed my family in the coming years. When I am well into my sixties, I might eat my grandfather's asparagus, perhaps with my children. Maybe they will eat it after I'm gone.

Radishes with Bacon Butter   serves 8

A plate of raw radishes served with soft butter and sea salt is a classic French hors d'oeuvre. I've added a trick I learned during a trip to Germany: beat some caraway-infused bacon fat into the butter. This recipe will give you an excuse to serve radishes for breakfast. They're also a great cocktail snack. Save the greens for Pasta with Radishes and Blue Cheese (page 54).

4 ounces bacon

½ teaspoon caraway seeds

1 stick unsalted butter, at room temperature

1 teaspoon lemon juice

Sea salt and black pepper

2 tablespoons finely chopped fresh flat-leaf parsley

1 small shallot, finely chopped

4 bunches radishes (about 2 pounds), trimmed, leaving 1 inch of stem

Pulse the bacon in a food processor until it is finely chopped or finely chop by hand. Cook the bacon in a 10-inch cast-iron or heavy skillet over medium heat, stirring occasionally, until it is browned, about 8 minutes. Stir in the caraway seeds and cook, stirring, until fragrant, 30 seconds to 1 minute. Remove from the heat and let the mixture cool to room temperature.

Beat the butter with an electric mixer in a medium bowl with the bacon mixture and any fat from the skillet, the lemon juice, ¾ teaspoon salt, and ¼ teaspoon pepper until the bacon butter is light and fluffy, about 5 minutes. Fold in the parsley and shallot and season to taste with salt and pepper.

Serve the radishes with the bacon butter.

Cold-Spring-Night Asparagus Soup serves 4 to 6

In most of the country, spring nights are still chilly enough for warming soups. This one is an appropriate bridge between winter and spring, and I like to sip it from a mug in front of one of the season's last crackling fires. It's hearty with chicken stock and a leek and bright from the herbs (dill and cilantro) and sour cream. Be generous with the sour cream. It lends a tangy richness to the soup.

1 large leek, pale green and white parts only

2 tablespoons unsalted butter

1 garlic clove, smashed

Kosher salt and black pepper

4 cups chicken stock or low-sodium broth

1 pound asparagus, trimmed

12 cilantro sprigs

6 fresh dill sprigs

Sour cream for serving

Slice the leeks crosswise and rinse under cold running water.

Melt the butter in a large heavy saucepan until the foam subsides. Cook the leek and garlic with ½ teaspoon each salt and pepper over medium heat, stirring occasionally, until the leek is soft but not browned, about 6 minutes. Add the stock and bring to a boil.

Cut the asparagus into 2-inch pieces, then add to the stock. Cook until tender, 6 to 10 minutes. Remove the pan from the heat and stir in the cilantro and dill. Transfer the soup to a blender in batches and blend until smooth. Season the soup with salt and pepper to taste. Serve topped with a dollop of sour cream.

Asparagus and Scrambled Egg
All-Day Breakfast Sandwiches serves 4

Friends who come to visit in the spring are always excited by the fresh air and the anticipation of the year's garden. Daytimes are filled with chores, but with a big group of friends pitching in, they go quickly, then we all sit down to a fresh home-cooked dinner. In the evening, we drink, dance, and blow off steam. My friend Alan Sytsma put this sandwich together one morning when we found ourselves with raging hangovers and a fridge full of leftovers. The cream cheese scrambled into the eggs adds a soothing richness.

8 ounces asparagus, trimmed
   and halved crosswise

1 tablespoon extra-virgin olive oil

¾ teaspoon kosher salt

½ teaspoon black pepper

4 sub or hoagie rolls

4 tablespoons mayonnaise

1 cup baby lettuce or arugula

6 large eggs

3 ounces cream cheese, cut into
   small cubes

1 tablespoon unsalted butter

Preheat the oven to 450°F.

Toss the asparagus with the oil, ½ teaspoon of the salt, and ¼ teaspoon of the pepper. Place on a baking sheet and roast in the oven for 15 minutes.

Split and toast the rolls, then spread them evenly with the mayonnaise and divide the lettuce among them.

Whisk together the eggs, cream cheese, and the remaining ¼ teaspoon each salt and pepper. Heat the butter in a large cast-iron or heavy nonstick skillet over medium heat until the foam subsides, add the eggs, and scramble the way you like them. (I prefer them on the wet side, which takes about 4 minutes.)

Divide the asparagus among the rolls, top with the eggs, and serve.

Spring Risotto serves 6

In this country-style risotto, ramps and mushrooms bring a woodsy earthiness, while the chicken stock provides a warming foundation. The ramps, tiny wild leeks that are native to the Northeast and parts of the Midwest, add a lot here, but scallions are a good substitute. Most risotto is finished with heavy cream and/or loads of butter. Not this one, which gets its creaminess (and a welcome brightness) from plain yogurt.

4 cups chicken stock or low-sodium broth

3 cups water

1 pound asparagus, trimmed

1 bunch ramps (see headnote) or scallions (about 4 ounces)

¼ cup extra-virgin olive oil

Kosher salt and black pepper

8 ounces sliced mushrooms (any kind)

2½ cups Arborio rice

¾ cup dry white wine

¾ cup finely grated Parmigiano-Reggiano

½ cup plain yogurt

2 tablespoons unsalted butter

2 tablespoons finely chopped fresh flat-leaf parsley

1 tablespoon Dijon mustard

Bring the stock and water to a simmer in a medium saucepan. Cut the asparagus into 2-inch pieces and simmer in the stock, uncovered, until just tender, about 4 minutes. Transfer the asparagus with a slotted spoon to an ice bath to stop cooking, then drain the asparagus. Keep the stock at a bare simmer, covered.

Finely chop the white- and lavender-colored ramp stems or the scallion whites, then cut the greens into 1-inch pieces and reserve them separately.

Heat the oil in a large heavy skillet over medium-high heat until it shimmers. Add the ramp stems or scallion whites, 1 teaspoon salt, and ½ teaspoon pepper and cook, stirring occasionally, until they are browned, 4 to 6 minutes. Add the mushrooms and continue to cook, stirring occasionally, until they are browned and any liquid they produce has evaporated, 6 to 8 minutes.

Add the rice, stirring to incorporate, then the wine. Cook, stirring frequently, until the wine is almost completely reduced. Add 1 cup of the stock, continuing to stir the rice frequently as it cooks. When the liquid is almost completely reduced, stir in another cup of the stock. Continue adding the stock and cooking the rice, stirring frequently, until the rice is tender, about 18 minutes for al dente rice or about 24 minutes for well-cooked rice.

When the rice reaches the texture you like, stir in the ramp or scallion greens, Parmesan, yogurt, butter, parsley, mustard, and the reserved asparagus. If you prefer a thinner risotto, add a little more stock. Season the risotto with salt and pepper to taste, and serve immediately.

Mustard-Garlic Chicken Paillards with Spring Peas and Lemon serves 4

Boneless, skinless chicken breasts can be bland, but paillards (just a French way of saying "flattened") cook so quickly that they retain a lot of flavor and stay really moist. The peas, mustard, and lemon zest pack a big punch into each juicy bite. If you can't grill, the paillards can be seared in a large hot skillet with a little oil.

For the peas

8 ounces snow peas

2 tablespoons extra-virgin olive oil

1 tablespoon unsalted butter

4 large scallions, finely chopped

1¼ pounds shell peas, shelled (1½ cups), or 1 (10-ounce) package frozen peas, thawed

1¼ teaspoons kosher salt

½ teaspoon black pepper

1 teaspoon finely grated lemon zest

2 teaspoons lemon juice

For the chicken

2 large garlic cloves

1¼ teaspoons kosher salt

3 tablespoons Dijon mustard

1 teaspoon finely grated lemon zest

½ teaspoon black pepper

4 boneless, skinless chicken breast halves (1¾ pounds total)

Pea shoots for garnish (optional)

Preheat the grill and oil the grill rack.

Make the peas: Trim the snow peas and cut them diagonally into thirds. Heat the oil and butter in a large heavy skillet over medium-high heat until the butter melts. Add the scallions and cook, stirring occasionally, until they start to brown, about 4 minutes. Add the snow peas, regular peas, salt, and pepper and cook, stirring occasionally, until the peas are tender and bright green, 3 to 5 minutes. Remove the skillet from the heat and stir in the lemon zest and juice. Keep warm.

Make the chicken: Mince and mash the garlic and ¼ teaspoon of the salt to a paste with a chef's knife. Stir together the garlic paste, mustard, lemon zest, the remaining 1 teaspoon salt, and the pepper in a medium bowl.

Place 1 chicken breast between two sheets of plastic wrap, then pound it with a meat pounder until it is ½ inch thick. Repeat with the remaining breasts. Rub the breasts all over with the mustard mixture.

Grill the chicken, turning once, until grill marks appear and it is cooked through, 3 to 4 minutes.

Serve the chicken topped with the pea mixture and fresh pea shoots, if desired.

Scallion-Rubbed Grilled Pork Tenderloin with Radish-Oregano Slaw serves 4

Scallions, radishes, and oregano are some of the first veggies and herbs to be ready in the early spring. And by then, I'm itching to break out the grill after a whole winter of letting it go un-used—that is, until I'm out there and realize it's still a little too cold to be cooking outside. No problem: pork tenderloins grill very quickly. By the time I'm chilly, they're done.

4 scallions, finely chopped

1 teaspoon cumin seeds

3 tablespoons lime juice

3 tablespoons extra-virgin olive oil

2½ teaspoons kosher salt

1¼ teaspoons black pepper

2 pork tenderloins (1½ pounds total)

1 bunch radishes (4–5 ounces)

1 tablespoon finely chopped shallot

1 tablespoon fresh oregano leaves

Stir together the scallions, cumin seeds, 1 tablespoon of the lime juice, 1 tablespoon of the oil, 2 teaspoons of the salt, and ¾ teaspoon of the pepper. Pat the tenderloins dry and marinate, chilled, in the scallion mixture for at least 30 minutes and up to 4 hours.

Preheat the grill and oil the grill rack.

Grill the pork, covered, turning occasionally, until an instant-read thermometer registers 145°F, 10 to 14 minutes. This temperature will produce slightly pink meat in the center of the tenderloins. If you prefer your pork more well-done, let the pork cook to 150°F, 12 to 16 minutes.

Transfer the pork to a cutting board and let it stand at room temperature for 10 minutes.

Trim the radishes and slice them very thinly with a slicer or a very sharp knife, then cut them into thin matchsticks. Toss the radishes with the shallot, oregano, the remaining 2 tablespoons lime juice, the remaining 2 tablespoons oil, and the remaining ½ teaspoon each salt and pepper.

Thinly slice the pork and serve with the radish slaw.

Garlic-Rubbed Boneless Leg of Lamb with Cucumber-Mint Sauce serves 8

Spark up the grill for this lamb on a not-quite-warm-enough afternoon, and within minutes you'll have a crowd gathering around its garlic-scented heat. The sauce is a fresh take on two different classic lamb-paired flavors: cucumbers are commonly used with lamb in Greek food, and mint sauce (read: jelly) is a classic English accompaniment. This dinner, which has become a standard spring (and Easter) dish in our family, combines them to surprising effect. If you're feeling ambitious, make the yogurt from scratch a day ahead using the recipe on page 101.

For the lamb

1 cup whole-milk yogurt (see headnote)

10 garlic cloves, finely chopped

2 tablespoons extra-virgin olive oil

1 tablespoon kosher salt

1 teaspoon black pepper

1 (8-pound) boneless leg of lamb (not tied)

For the sauce

1 English cucumber (not peeled)

½ cup fresh mint leaves

¼ cup sugar

1 teaspoon finely grated lemon zest

3 tablespoons lemon juice

2 tablespoons extra-virgin olive oil

1 teaspoon kosher salt

½ teaspoon black pepper

Make the lamb: Stir together the yogurt, garlic, oil, salt, and pepper. Pat the lamb dry and pierce all over with a paring knife. Rub the lamb with the garlic mixture and marinate, chilled, for at least 30 minutes and up to 2 hours.

Preheat the grill and oil the grill rack.

Grill the lamb, covered, turning occasionally, until an instant-read thermometer inserted in the thickest part registers 135°F for medium-rare (keeping in mind that the temperature will rise 10° to 15°F later, when it rests), 20 to 25 minutes. Transfer the lamb to a cutting board and let it stand at room temperature for 20 minutes.

Make the sauce: Chop the cucumber and place it in a food processor with the mint, sugar, lemon zest, juice, oil, salt, and pepper. Pulse until the sauce is combined but still chunky.

Slice the lamb and serve with the cucumber-mint sauce.

Asparagus and Baby Potato Roast serves 4

This side dish is so simple to make that you might pass it over, but don't! The quick roasting time together with the fresh flavor of the vinaigrette will make this a spring staple at your house. Giving the potatoes a head start allows them to crisp up and finish cooking at the same time as the asparagus. You'll have extra room left in your oven for the rest of the dinner — like Garlic-Pesto Roast Chicken (page 55).

1 pound small potatoes, cut into ½-inch slices

3 tablespoons extra-virgin olive oil

Kosher salt and black pepper

1 pound asparagus, trimmed

1½ tablespoons white wine vinegar

1 tablespoon finely chopped shallot

2 teaspoons finely chopped fresh tarragon

Preheat the oven to 400°F.

Toss the potatoes with 2 tablespoons of the oil, ½ teaspoon salt, and ¼ teaspoon pepper. Place on a baking sheet and roast in the oven for 15 minutes.

Cut the asparagus into thirds and toss with the remaining 1 tablespoon oil, ½ teaspoon salt, and ¼ teaspoon pepper. After the potatoes have roasted for 15 minutes, scatter the asparagus onto the baking sheet with the potatoes and return to the oven. Continue to roast for 15 minutes more.

Stir together the vinegar, shallot, and tarragon.

When the potatoes are browned and tender and the asparagus is tender, toss with the vinegar mixture, season with salt and pepper to taste, and serve.

Grilled Asparagus and Shaved Fennel Tangle serves 4

I'll never understand why fennel remains so underrated. Cut thin, it requires no cooking whatsoever. Mixed with grilled asparagus and mint, it's an all-out ode to spring. The black and green olives and mozzarella in this salad make the flavor of these veggies pop. If you can find bocconcini (mini mozzarella balls), substitute them for the chopped mozzarella. I first made this salad for a late lunch with my father. Dad always loves to fire up the grill, even if he's just grilling asparagus. He's right to do so: the char adds a ton of flavor to the dish.

1 pound asparagus, trimmed

3 tablespoons extra-virgin olive oil

Kosher salt and black pepper

1 medium head fennel, with some fronds

⅓ cup chopped pitted green and black olives

8 ounces chopped fresh mozzarella (see headnote)

3 tablespoons finely chopped fresh mint

Preheat the grill.

Toss the asparagus with the oil, ½ teaspoon salt, and ¼ teaspoon pepper in a shallow bowl. Lift the asparagus out of the bowl, letting the excess oil drain back into the bowl. Grill the asparagus, turning occasionally, until it is tender, about 8 minutes for thin asparagus and about 12 minutes for thick.

Thinly shave the fennel bulb with a slicer or a very sharp knife, then toss it with the oil remaining in the bowl.

Toss the asparagus with the fennel, olives, mozzarella, mint, ½ teaspoon salt, and ¼ teaspoon pepper. Tear some fennel fronds and sprinkle over the dish. Season with salt and pepper to taste and serve.

Beet and Snap Pea Salad with Ricotta serves 6

Most people wouldn't think of serving beets raw, but here they act as a flavor foundation to the fresh snap peas. At first, you may be irritated that your hands turn red from handling the beets, but when your friends start raving about this dish, you'll be glad to have proof that you were the one who made it. Toasting the walnuts in the oil brings a nutty flavor to the dressing that really makes the dish.

Black walnut trees grow all over the farm. Their nuts are more intense than those available at the supermarket, but their shells are a virtual fortress. You'll need a hammer to crack them open. For me, it's worth the effort, but if you are afraid of missing the nut and whacking your thumb, store-bought walnuts are a fine stand-in.

½ cup black walnuts or regular walnuts

¼ cup extra-virgin olive oil

1 pound sugar snap peas (4 cups)

1 pound assorted beets with some greens attached, such as red, golden, Chioggia, and/or white

¼ cup finely chopped fresh mint, plus some leaves for garnish

3 tablespoons balsamic vinegar

Kosher salt and black pepper

¾ cup fresh ricotta (see page 22)

Toast the walnuts in the oil in a small skillet until they are pale golden, 2 to 3 minutes. Let the nut oil cool completely.

Trim the sugar snaps, then cook them in a saucepan of boiling salted water until they are just bright green, about 2 minutes. Drain the snap peas and transfer them to an ice bath to cool, drain them again, and pat them dry. Thinly slice the snap peas diagonally and transfer them to a large bowl.

Trim the beets, leaving about 1 inch of stem. Peel the beets with a vegetable peeler, then, using the stems as handles, slice them as thinly as possible with a slicer or a sharp knife. Cut the slices into very thin matchsticks. Add the beets to the bowl with the snap peas.

Toss in the chopped mint, vinegar, nuts (with the oil), 1½ teaspoons salt, and ¾ teaspoon pepper. Season with additional salt and pepper to taste, scatter the mint leaves and dollops of ricotta over the top or on the side and serve.

Watercress and Radish Salad with Pennsylvania Pickled Eggs salad serves 4 to 6; makes 12 eggs

As a native Pennsylvanian, I grew up eating beet-pickled eggs. They are sold at many farmers' markets in the state and in big glass jars at local bars. It's about time they caught on in the rest of the country, too. I like them when they have marinated for just a few hours in the beet-pickling liquid, but if you prefer a deeper pickled flavor (and a slightly bouncier texture), keep the eggs in the brine for up to 3 days. They are a great snack when you're slugging down a few beers or just want a quick bite. Here they add color and flavor to a simple spring salad that uses the pickling liquid in place of vinegar.

For the eggs

3 cups water

1 cup apple cider vinegar or distilled white vinegar

1 small beet, peeled and quartered

1 shallot, sliced

1 tablespoon sugar

2 teaspoons kosher salt

12 hard-boiled eggs (see opposite page), peeled

For the salad

4 radishes

1 teaspoon Dijon mustard

1 tablespoon egg-pickling liquid or distilled white vinegar

2 tablespoons extra-virgin olive oil

Kosher salt and black pepper

1 pound watercress (about 2 bunches)

Make the eggs: Bring the water, vinegar, beet, shallot, sugar, and salt to a boil in a small saucepan and boil until the beet is tender, about 20 minutes. Cool the liquid completely, then place the eggs in a large glass or plastic container and cover with the pickling liquid. Chill the eggs, stirring once or twice for even coloring, for 3 hours. The eggs will keep in the pickling liquid for at least a week, but their texture will become rubbery. If you prefer softer eggs (as I do), remove them from the pickling liquid and keep them refrigerated.

Make the salad: Slice the radishes very thinly with a slicer or a very sharp knife.

Whisk together the mustard, pickling liquid, oil, ½ teaspoon salt, and ¼ teaspoon pepper in a large bowl. Toss the watercress and radishes with the dressing. Slice 4 or 5 eggs crosswise and gently toss with the salad. (Reserve the remaining eggs for another use.) Season with salt and pepper to taste and serve.

The Perfect Hard-Boiled Egg

Hard-boiled eggs are harder to get right than you might think. Eggs' proteins coagulate (become firm) somewhere around 160°F. If they get too hot for too long, they become rubbery and the yolks become greenish. Remember, a perfect hard-boiled egg is never boiled hard, just gently and briefly simmered.

Place your eggs in a saucepan and cover them with room-temperature water (hot water on cold eggs causes the shells to crack). Place the saucepan over high heat and bring the water to a gentle simmer. Remove the saucepan from the heat and cover it. Let stand for 10 minutes. Since water retains heat well, it will gently cook the eggs all the way through, producing tender whites and bright yellow yolks. After 10 minutes, remove the eggs from the water and rinse them under cold running water for about a minute to make them easier to peel. Once cooked, the eggs keep in the refrigerator for at least 3 weeks.

Creamed Watercress serves 4 to 6

Similar to creamed spinach, this is a perfect side for any spring meal, from a simple weeknight dinner to an extravagant Easter feast. I learned the technique from my friend Ruth Reichl, who published a similar recipe in *Garlic and Sapphires*. Hers has more butter and does not use the mascarpone cheese. In both versions, potato contributes body to the dish. It's a thrifty and clever way to add a little more richness, too. If you can't find mascarpone, substitute cream cheese.

½ medium Yukon Gold potato, peeled

Kosher salt

1½ pounds watercress (about 3 bunches)

2 tablespoons unsalted butter

¼ cup mascarpone cheese

Black pepper

Cut the potato into ½-inch pieces. Cover the potato with water in a medium pot and add 1 teaspoon salt. Bring to a boil and cook until the potato is very tender, 15 to 20 minutes. Remove the potato with a slotted spoon, transferring it to a food processor. Bring the water back to a boil, add the watercress, and blanch until it is bright green, about 1 minute. Transfer the watercress to a colander and press on it to remove as much liquid as possible. Puree the watercress in the food processor with the potato, butter, mascarpone, ½ teaspoon salt, and ½ teaspoon pepper. Season with salt and pepper to taste and serve.

Strawberry-Rhubarb Fool Shortcake serves 12

Fool is an old-fashioned dessert made by folding pureed fruit into whipped cream. This recipe combines the flavors of strawberry and rhubarb with the familiar base of shortcake. I made it the first time to celebrate my cousin Leif's college graduation. It was such a hit that everyone asked me for the recipe.

For the biscuits

3 cups cake flour

1½ tablespoons baking powder

1½ teaspoons kosher salt

1¾ cups heavy cream, plus more for brushing

For the fool

2 pounds rhubarb

¾ cup sugar

2 teaspoons minced fresh ginger

1 vanilla bean, split lengthwise

1½ cups heavy cream

For the strawberries

1 quart strawberries

¼ cup sugar

2 tablespoons orange liqueur

Preheat the oven to 425°F, with a rack in the middle. Lightly butter a baking sheet.

Make the biscuits: Whisk together the flour, baking powder, and salt in a bowl. Add the cream and stir just until a dough forms. Gently knead the dough in the bowl until it just comes together. Pat the dough out on a lightly floured work surface to a ½-inch thickness. Cut as many 3-inch rounds from the dough as possible, transferring them to the baking sheet. Gather the scraps and re-form the remaining dough, cutting out more rounds; you will have 12 to 15 biscuits. Brush the tops of the biscuits with cream, then bake until golden, 15 to 20 minutes.

Let the biscuits cool completely on a rack.

Make the fool: Cut the rhubarb into 1-inch pieces, discarding any leaves. Combine the rhubarb, sugar, and ginger in a medium saucepan. Scrape the seeds from the vanilla bean and add the seeds and pod to the rhubarb mixture. Cook the rhubarb until it is very soft and falling apart, stirring occasionally, about 12 minutes. Let the rhubarb cool completely, then remove the vanilla pod.

Make the strawberries: Hull the strawberries and cut them in half. Toss them with the sugar and liqueur, letting them macerate at room temperature for at least 30 minutes.

Just before serving, whip the cream until it holds soft peaks. Fold the cooled rhubarb into the cream. Split the biscuits in half. Top the bottoms of the biscuits with the rhubarb fool and strawberries. Cap with the biscuit tops and serve with some of the strawberry liquid.

Mary's Lemon Sponge Pie serves 6 to 8

Hunting through old family recipes one day, I came across this pie, written on an index card in my grandmother's handwriting. The crust is standard, but the filling is extra-special, though it is made from nothing more than pantry items: lemons, eggs, milk, sugar, and flour. Beaten egg whites add a wonderful, fluffy texture.

For the pastry dough

1¼ cups all-purpose flour

1 stick unsalted butter, cut into cubes

1 teaspoon light or dark brown sugar

½ teaspoon kosher salt

2–3 tablespoons cold water

For the filling

1 cup sugar

3 tablespoons unsalted butter, melted

2 large eggs, separated

3 tablespoons all-purpose flour

1 teaspoon finely grated lemon zest

6 tablespoons lemon juice

Pinch of kosher salt

1 cup whole milk

Make the pastry dough: Work together the flour, butter, brown sugar, and salt in a medium bowl with your hands until the mixture is mostly combined, but with some small lumps of butter remaining. Stir in 2 tablespoons of the water with a fork. Press a small handful of dough together: if it looks powdery and does not come together, stir in the remaining 1 tablespoon water. Transfer the dough to a sheet of plastic wrap. Using the edge of the plastic, fold the dough over on itself, pressing until it comes together. Form the dough into a disk, wrap completely in the plastic, and chill for 1 hour.

Preheat the oven to 450°F, with a rack in the middle.

On a well-floured surface, roll out the pastry dough with a floured rolling pin into an 11-inch round. Place the dough in a 9-inch pie tin and crimp the edges.

Make the filling: Whisk together the sugar, butter, egg yolks, flour, lemon zest, juice, and salt in a medium bowl. Whisk in the milk. Beat the egg whites until they hold soft peaks, then gently fold the whites into the lemon mixture.

Pour the filling into the pie shell and bake for 10 minutes. Lower the oven temperature to 350°F and continue to bake until the filling is set, about 35 minutes more. Cool slightly on a rack. Serve warm or at room temperature.

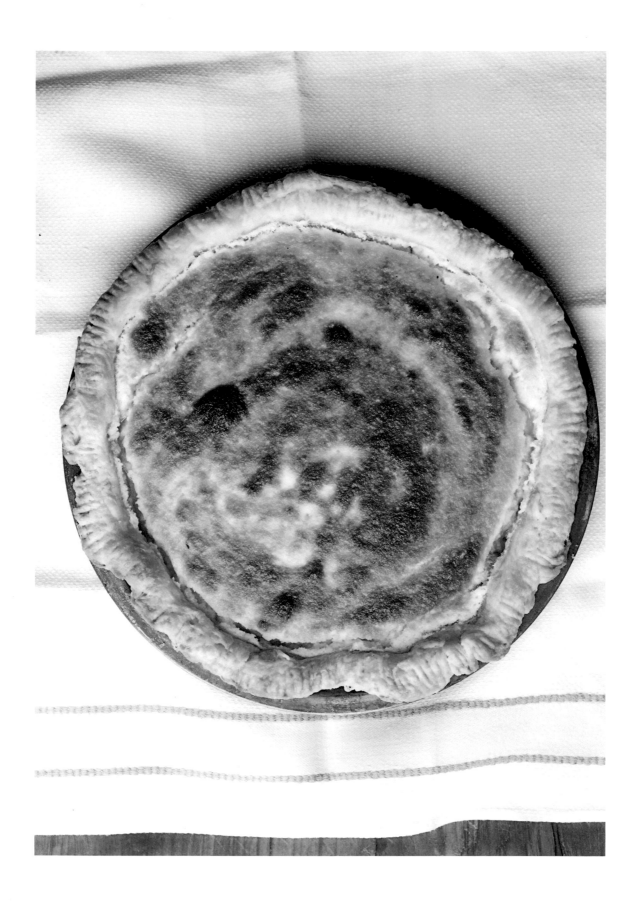

A New Link in the Chain

ARLY JUNE marked Makaila's first visit to the farm. She was born in April to my cousin Leif and his wife, Megan. When Leif proudly pulled her from the back seat of the car, the baby's eyes squinted and adjusted to the big open sky. She smiled, then cried, then smiled again as Leif passed her around the circle of admiring cousins. Watching him hold Makaila cuddled in his tattooed forearms and nuzzled with his scruffy beard was like seeing a real-life *Beauty and the Beast*. Leif's parents, my aunt and uncle, once brought him here for the first time, as my parents did with me, as did their parents with them.

Leif has a restlessness that drives him. The inability to sit still is a family trait. So is the ability to sustain fairly serious injuries that inevitably happen as a result of the long list of farm chores. As Megan, my sisters Cecily and Haley, and other friends passed Makaila around, Leif and I chained a fallen tree to the back of his truck and started to drag it down the hill toward the firewood pile. When we reached about fifteen miles an hour, Leif glanced in his rearview mirror and yelled, "Uh-oh." Just then the truck jerked to a stop, as the tree we were dragging caught on another tree. My head jolted forward, cracking the windshield. I went to ice down my skull while he finished the chore. About the time my head stopped hurting, he had finished mowing the lawn, trimming some trees, and feeding Makaila.

We were all starting to get hungry when Leif asked for a tour of the garden, where Cecily and I pointed out the abundance of dinner options. We gathered armfuls of velvety-leaved lettuces, bunches of cilantro, and handfuls of fragile young green beans. The radishes were almost too big, but we picked them anyway, shaking dirt back into the holes they'd pushed into the ground.

We brainstormed about a new way to make chicken wings and decided to put the fresh-picked cilantro to use in the sauce. Everyone devoured our creation, licking the bones clean, while we talked about what else we might eat. Leif was intrigued by my idea of cooking the radishes. We headed into the kitchen as my parents' car rolled slowly down the lane toward the farmhouse.

Cecily and her husband, Dave, set a table on the porch, using chairs and a bench from the house. Haley picked wildflowers and placed them in the center of the table. Leif and I drank beer and sliced garlic scapes and washed lettuce. Leif, whose knife of choice is a bowie not a chef's, asked me for a quick lesson in how to chop an onion. Soon we all sat down to pasta with radishes and blue cheese, quickly sautéed green beans, and buttery lettuce salad with an herb-heavy dressing, all served family-style.

My father took a bite of salad and put down his fork. He said it was the best lettuce he'd eaten in years. It was the best lettuce I'd eaten, maybe ever; it popped in my mouth and was nutty, sweet, crisp, and buttery. It tasted more like lettuce than anything I'd ever eaten, including lettuce. I had thirds of salad. The lettuce alone had made the work of the garden worthwhile.

After dinner my parents drove back to their house, and the rest of us sat on the porch, listening to the frogs sing in the pond. We drank wine and talked about the list of chores my father had left for us to complete. Leif joked that I might want to wear a helmet when we worked. The work would be far too much for one or two people, but together, we'd finish by late afternoon, just in time for another dinner from the garden.

Spicy Cilantro Chicken Wings serves 4 to 6

Everyone loves chicken wings, that fiery and buttery all-American snack that pairs perfectly with lots and lots of beer. I love adding unexpected flavors to familiar foods, and these wings are a perfect example of why it's fun to think outside the bottle of Frank's hot sauce. The chile, lime, garlic, cilantro, and Worcestershire provide a savory-acidic base for the sauce and add many new and wonderful layers of flavor, while the butter coats the wings with a luscious richness.

When you break out a bowl of green-hued wings during dinner or while watching the big game, your guests might be fooled into thinking they won't pack a punch. My advice: play along and let them sweat it out — they'll come back for more, thanks to the perfect balance of bright lime juice, soft butter, and fiery spice.

⅓ cup chopped cilantro stems

1½ teaspoons finely grated lime zest

3 tablespoons lime juice

2 tablespoons Worcestershire sauce

1 hot green chile, such as habanero, serrano, or Thai, chopped

1 large garlic clove, chopped

1¾ teaspoons kosher salt

½ teaspoon black pepper

½ stick unsalted butter, melted

3 pounds chicken wings

About 4 cups vegetable oil for frying

Cilantro leaves

Puree the cilantro stems, lime zest, juice, Worcestershire, chile, garlic, ¾ teaspoon of the salt, and the pepper in a blender until smooth. With the motor running, add the butter, blending until it is incorporated. Transfer the sauce to a large bowl.

Pat the wings dry, then halve them at the joint and season them with the remaining 1 teaspoon salt.

Heat 1 inch of oil in a pot or deep heavy skillet to 400°F. Fry the wings in 2 or 3 batches, turning occasionally, until they are golden and cooked through, about 8 minutes per batch (return the oil to 400°F between batches). As they are cooked, transfer the wings to the bowl with the sauce, tossing them to coat, or serve the sauce on the side for dipping. With tongs or a slotted spoon, transfer the wings to a serving plate and sprinkle with the cilantro leaves. Serve the wings with the remaining sauce on the side.

Pasta with Garlic-Scape Pesto

serves 6 to 8 (makes 1½ cups pesto)

Garlic scapes are the soft, lime-green-colored stems and unopened flower buds of hard-neck garlic varieties. Scapes have a mild garlic flavor and a slight sweetness, which makes them a prized addition in the kitchen. You can find them in the early summer and midfall at farmers' markets. If you grow your own garlic (which is easy), trim the scapes off before their flowers open. This forces the plant to focus on bulb production and increases the size of the garlic cloves.

My Aunt Denise introduced me to the idea of garlic-scape pesto. Here I use it to sauce pasta; you can also spread it on crostini or use as a pungent dip for crunchy vegetables. If all you have are salted pistachios, forgo the salt in the recipe and add salt to taste at the end.

For the pesto

10 large garlic scapes

⅓ cup unsalted pistachios (see headnote)

⅓ cup finely grated Parmigiano-Reggiano

Kosher salt and black pepper

⅓ cup extra-virgin olive oil

1 pound spaghetti

Make the pesto: Puree the garlic scapes, pistachios, Parmesan, ½ teaspoon salt, and ¼ teaspoon pepper in a food processor until very finely chopped. With the motor running, slowly pour the oil through the opening. Season the pesto with salt and pepper to taste. (The pesto keeps in the fridge, covered, for 1 week or frozen for a month.)

In a large pot of heavily salted boiling water, cook the spaghetti until al dente. Reserve 1 cup of the pasta-cooking water, then drain the pasta. Whisk together ⅔ cup of the pesto and the reserved pasta water and toss with the pasta. Season with salt and pepper to taste and serve right away.

Pasta with Radishes and Blue Cheese   serves 4

Waste nothing: at the farm, we take that adage seriously. Trimmed grapevines work as kindling in the winter, used beeswax becomes candles, and vegetable greens turn into dinner. Don't throw out your radish greens (especially if you're making Radishes with Bacon Butter, page 28). Instead, toss them in some pasta and make a meal out of an ingredient that might have otherwise ended up in the compost heap. The blue cheese melts with the heat of the pasta and becomes a savory sauce.

Kosher salt

4 bunches radish greens
   (6 ounces)

4 slices bacon, chopped

2 tablespoons extra-virgin olive oil

1 onion, chopped

5 garlic cloves, sliced

Black pepper

8 ounces crumbled mild blue
   cheese

2 tablespoons unsalted butter
   or cream

1 bunch radishes (without greens;
   4 ounces)

1 pound spaghetti

1 cup toasted bread crumbs

In a large pot of heavily salted boiling water, cook the greens until they are tender but still have chew and are bright green, about 1 minute. Transfer the greens to a colander with a slotted spoon and, when they are cool enough to touch, press on them to remove most of the liquid. Bring the water back to a boil.

Cook the bacon with the oil in a large heavy skillet over medium heat until the bacon just starts to brown, about 5 minutes. Add the onion and garlic with ½ teaspoon each salt and pepper and cook, stirring occasionally, until the onion is golden, 8 to 10 minutes. Remove from the heat and add the greens, blue cheese, and butter.

Thinly slice the radishes.

Boil the pasta until it is al dente. Reserve about 1 cup of the pasta-cooking water. Drain the pasta, then add it to the skillet, tossing with tongs. Add some of the reserved water for a thinner sauce, then season to taste with salt and pepper.

Top the dish with the bread crumbs and the radishes and serve immediately.

Garlic-Pesto Roast Chicken   serves 4

We eat a lot of roast chicken at the farm. It's inexpensive, easy, and always feeds a happy crowd. During the time I spent in the test kitchens of *Gourmet*, I discovered an amazing method for a superjuicy bird with perfectly crisp skin: the secret is a hot oven and turning the bird to mimic a rotisserie. The results are shockingly moist. This simple, flavorful version uses Garlic-Scape Pesto. (You can substitute store-bought pesto, but the results won't be nearly as good.) If serving with Kielbasa Roast Potatoes (page 63), use only one roasting pan and scatter the potatoes around the chicken. Any leftover chicken meat can be mixed with a little mayonnaise for a killer chicken salad.

1 (3½-pound) chicken

¼ cup Garlic-Scape Pesto (page 52)

1¼ teaspoons kosher salt

1 teaspoon black pepper

1 lemon, halved

Preheat the oven to 450°F, with a rack in the middle.

Rinse the chicken and pat it dry. Being careful not to tear the skin, start at the large cavity and gently run your fingers between the skin and the meat to loosen the skin. Push the pesto under the skin, including around the thighs and drumsticks, and massage the skin from outside to spread the pesto evenly.

Season the chicken inside and out with the salt and pepper. Place the lemon halves in the cavity and loosely tie the legs together with kitchen string. Place the chicken in a roasting pan on its side (one wing up; you may need to lean the chicken against the side of the pan) and roast for 15 minutes. Turn the chicken over to the other side using tongs, and continue to roast for 15 minutes more. Turn the chicken onto its back and continue to roast until it is golden and the skin starts to pull away from the base of the drumsticks, another 20 to 25 minutes. Transfer the chicken to a cutting board and let it rest for 15 minutes before carving and serving.

Honey-Jalapeño Chicken Tenders serves 6 to 8

My friend Michelli came up with this simple recipe one early-summer afternoon as a way to use up a big pile of chilcs and some honey that I had recently taken from the beehive. The dish soon became a favorite. Chicken tenders cook very quickly, which helps keep them juicy, and the honey in the recipe caramelizes in no time. Remove the jalapeño seeds for a less spicy version. If you don't want to grill the tenders, they can be broiled about 5 inches from the heat for about 6 minutes.

¼ cup honey

3 tablespoons soy sauce

2 tablespoons extra-virgin olive oil

4 garlic cloves, minced

6 jalapeño peppers, finely chopped

1 tablespoon finely grated lemon zest

2 teaspoons kosher salt

¾ teaspoon black pepper

3 pounds chicken tenders

½ cup chopped fresh cilantro

Sour cream for serving

Preheat the grill and oil the grill rack.

Whisk together the honey, soy sauce, oil, garlic, jalapeños, lemon zest, salt, and pepper. Toss the chicken in the marinade and let stand for at least 10 minutes.

Grill the chicken until well browned and cooked through, 4 to 6 minutes. Serve the chicken sprinkled with the cilantro and with a dollop of sour cream on the plate.

Grilled Chorizo with Corn and Bell Pepper Salsa   serves 6

Fresh chorizo sausage is available at many supermarkets and adds a huge amount of flavor to any cookout. (You'll need the Mexican-style, not the dried Spanish version.) The smokiness and spiciness of the sausage are a perfect backdrop for sweet corn and peppers. (By the way, this is also one of my favorite summer "hot dogs"—place the chorizo in a toasted bun, then top with the corn salsa and a little mayonnaise.) The quick and easy salsa makes for a great topping.

For the salsa

4 ears corn (with husks)

1 red or orange bell pepper

½ cup crumbled cotija or ricotta salata cheese

1 tablespoon lime juice

2 tablespoons extra-virgin olive oil

Kosher salt and black pepper

6 fresh chorizo sausages

Preheat the grill.

Make the salsa: Place the corn ears in their husks over indirect heat on the grill and cook them, covered, until the kernels are tender, about 30 minutes. Turn off the grill, if using gas. Let the corn cool, then husk and cut off the kernels. Finely chop the pepper and toss with the corn, cheese, lime juice, oil, ½ teaspoon salt, and ½ teaspoon pepper. Season the salsa with salt and pepper to taste.

Light the gas grill or add more charcoal if necessary. Place the chorizo on the grill over direct heat. Cook the sausages, turning occasionally, until grill marks appear and they are cooked through, 10 to 14 minutes. Serve the chorizo with the corn salsa.

Seared Cowboy Steaks
with Guinness Sauce   serves 6 (or 4 cowboys)

My cousin Leif is a Guinness fan and is always willing to split a pint of creamy stout. One cold spring evening, he and I got the idea to make a Guinness sauce for a steak. Luckily, the sauce used only half a cup of the beer, and Leif was more than happy to finish the pint.

The steak was a rib-eye on the trimmed bone, the cut that old-time butchers call a cowboy steak. You can pick it up by the bone and feel like Fred Flintstone, but it's a lot of meat and will feed two or three noncowboys. Leif and I like to think we're pretty tough, but these steaks were too much to handle for dinner. There was steak and eggs for breakfast the next morning and cleaned bones for the dogs.

2 bone-in rib-eye steaks (2–2½ inches thick; 2–2½ pounds each)

2 teaspoons kosher salt

1 teaspoon black pepper

1 tablespoon extra-virgin olive oil or Master Fat (page 23)

1 large shallot, thinly sliced

2 garlic cloves, finely chopped

1 tablespoon tomato paste

½ cup Guinness or other Irish stout

½ cup beef stock or low-sodium broth

1 tablespoon Worcestershire sauce

½ stick unsalted butter

Preheat the oven to 400°F.

Season the steaks with the salt and pepper. Heat the oil in a large heavy ovenproof skillet (preferably cast-iron) over medium heat until it shimmers. Sear the steaks on both sides, then brown on the fat side (opposite the bone), about 6 minutes total. Transfer the skillet to the oven and roast until the steaks register 110°F in the center with an instant-read thermometer for medium-rare (the steaks' temperature will rise as they rest; for medium, leave the steaks in the oven for another 5 minutes, or until they reach 115°F). This will take about 30 minutes. Transfer the steaks to a cutting board and let them rest for at least 10 minutes.

Pour off all but 2 tablespoons fat from the skillet (add to your Master Fat), then add the shallot and garlic and cook over medium heat, stirring, until the garlic is golden brown, about 2 minutes. Add the tomato paste and cook, stirring, until the tomato paste starts to brown, about 1 minute. Add the Guinness and boil until the liquid is almost completely reduced, about 2 minutes. Add the beef stock and Worcestershire sauce, then boil until the liquid is reduced by about half, 2 to 3 minutes. Remove the skillet from the heat and whisk in the butter. Serve the steaks with the Guinness sauce.

Green Salad with Green Goddess Dressing serves 6 to 8 (makes about 1¾ cups dressing)

Green goddess is one of my all-time favorite dressings. Sort of like ranch dressing but sophisticated, not only is it a perfect dressing for a big green salad but it can be used as a dip for just about anything (French fries and chicken wings top my list). Try tossing steamed green beans or a head of roasted cauliflower with green goddess, and you'll have a dish that will clear plates. Drizzle it on beets, smear it on sandwiches, put it on your burger, and serve it with fried chicken.

Why is it so delicious? The secret is the anchovy fillets. They add a deep base of flavor without taking over. Feel free to experiment with different mixes of herbs. I prefer to go heavy on the dill and tarragon, but have fun with it to see what best matches your taste. No matter what combination of herbs you choose, use lots and lots of them.

1 small shallot

1 small garlic clove, chopped

2 anchovy fillets

½ cup mayonnaise

½ cup buttermilk

⅓ cup chopped fresh flat-leaf parsley

¼ cup chopped fresh dill

¼ cup chopped fresh tarragon

2 scallions, chopped

2 tablespoons apple cider vinegar

Kosher salt and black pepper

2 heads Boston (butter) lettuce, torn

Pulse the shallot, garlic, and anchovies in a food processor until finely chopped. Add the mayonnaise, buttermilk, parsley, dill, tarragon, scallions, vinegar, ½ teaspoon salt, and ¼ teaspoon pepper and pulse until the herbs are finely chopped. Toss the lettuce with enough dressing to coat the leaves. Season the salad with salt and pepper to taste. Any remaining dressing keeps in the refrigerator, covered, for 1 week.

Green Beans with Garlic Chips and Olive Oil   serves 4 to 6

I'm always looking for new ways to cook green beans, since my plants produce throughout the summer. This is one of those recipes I made on the fly when I had plenty of beans and garlic on hand. Now people request it all the time. A ton of garlic gives this dish seriously deep flavor, and the chips add a nice crunch.

3 tablespoons extra-virgin olive oil

5 garlic cloves, thinly sliced lengthwise

1 tablespoon unsalted butter

1 red onion, sliced

Kosher salt and black pepper

1 pound young green beans, trimmed

2 tablespoons apple cider vinegar

Heat the oil with the garlic in a heavy skillet over medium heat. Cook, stirring occasionally, until the garlic is golden, 5 to 6 minutes. Remove the garlic with a slotted spoon, transferring to a paper towel.

Add the butter to the oil in the skillet and increase the heat to medium-high. Add the onion, 1½ teaspoons salt, and ¾ teaspoon pepper and sauté, stirring, until the onion is golden, about 6 minutes.

Add the beans and continue to sauté, stirring occasionally, until tender, about 5 minutes. Stir in the vinegar and season with salt and pepper to taste.

Transfer the beans to a serving dish and sprinkle with the garlic chips.

Turnip Reunion serves 4 to 6

Many people don't realize that young turnips grow quickly and bring with them a wonderful freebie in the form of their greens, which are easy to cook and very tasty. One June evening, my cousin Leif volunteered to help cook dinner. We collected turnips from the garden, cooked them and their greens separately, and then served them together on the same plate. "It's a turnip reunion," he said. Be sure to wash the greens well. They grow in dirt.

5 large turnips with greens

2 tablespoons unsalted butter

1 cup water

Kosher salt and black pepper

1 small onion, finely chopped

2 tablespoons extra-virgin olive oil

1 tablespoon hot sauce, such as
    Valentina or Frank's

Trim and peel the turnips (reserve the greens), then cut them into 1½-inch wedges. Heat the butter in a large heavy skillet over medium heat until the foam subsides, then add the turnips and cook, stirring occasionally, until they are browned, 4 to 6 minutes. Add the water to the skillet, along with ¾ teaspoon salt and ½ teaspoon pepper, cover, and boil until the turnips are very soft, 10 to 12 minutes. Uncover and continue to boil until all the liquid has evaporated, about 5 minutes. Season the turnips with salt and pepper to taste, transfer to a serving plate, and keep warm. Wipe out the skillet.

Meanwhile, trim the greens, discarding any thick stems, and rinse well. Plunge the leaves into a large pot of well-salted boiling water and cook until tender, 5 to 8 minutes. Drain the leaves in a colander, and when they are cool enough to touch, press out any extra liquid. Coarsely chop the leaves.

Cook the onion in the oil in the skillet over medium-high heat until browned, 6 to 8 minutes. Add the greens and hot sauce, stirring to combine. Season the greens with salt and pepper to taste and serve them with the turnips.

Kielbasa Roast Potatoes   serves 4

I love kielbasa and keep a ring of it in the fridge at all times. It's one of the easiest ways to add porky, smoky flavor to any dish. Potatoes are natural flavor sponges and soak up the juices of the sausage. These potatoes are terrific served with Garlic-Pesto Roast Chicken (page 55). If you make them for the same meal, roast the potatoes and the chicken in the same pan, scattering the potatoes and kielbasa around the chicken and roasting them for the same amount of time as the chicken (50 to 55 minutes). The chicken juices will prevent the potatoes and kielbasa from scorching.

2 pounds waxy potatoes, such as Yukon Gold or Red Bliss

8 ounces kielbasa, sliced into ½-inch rounds

1 tablespoon extra-virgin olive oil

2 fresh thyme sprigs

¾ teaspoon kosher salt

½ teaspoon black pepper

Preheat the oven to 450°F, with a rack in the middle.

Wash the potatoes and cut them into bite-sized pieces. Toss the potatoes in a large roasting pan with the kielbasa, oil, thyme, salt, and pepper.

Roast the potatoes, stirring once, until they are browned and soft, 30 to 40 minutes. Transfer to a serving dish and serve.

Strawberry–Cream Cheese Pie serves 6 to 8

My Aunt Janet sent me this recipe for my grandmother's strawberry pie. It ended up being a huge hit with everyone who tried it. When I raved about it to my aunt, she told me that it works just as well with fresh blueberries.

For the pastry dough

1¼ cups all-purpose flour

1 stick unsalted butter, cut into cubes

1 teaspoon light or dark brown sugar

½ teaspoon kosher salt

2–3 tablespoons cold water

For the filling

1 quart strawberries, trimmed

¾ cup sugar

3 tablespoons cornstarch

2 tablespoons lemon juice

3 ounces cream cheese, at room temperature

Lightly whipped cream for serving

Make the pastry dough: Work together the flour, butter, brown sugar, and salt in a medium bowl with your hands until the mixture is mostly combined, with some small lumps of butter remaining. Stir in 2 tablespoons of the water with a fork. Press a small handful of dough together; if it looks powdery and does not come together, stir in the remaining 1 tablespoon water. Transfer the dough to a sheet of plastic wrap. Using the edge of the plastic, fold the dough over on itself, pressing until it comes together. Form the dough into a disk, wrap completely in the plastic, and chill for 1 hour.

Preheat the oven to 400°F, with a rack in the middle.

On a well-floured surface, roll out the pastry dough with a floured rolling pin into an 11-inch round. Place the dough in a 9-inch pie tin and crimp the edges. Place a sheet of parchment paper or foil over the dough, then fill with pie weights or dried beans. Bake the crust until set, about 25 minutes. Remove the pie weights and the parchment paper and continue to bake until the crust is golden, another 10 to 15 minutes. Let the pie shell cool to room temperature.

Make the filling: Mash half of the strawberries with the sugar, cornstarch, and lemon juice. Place the strawberry mixture in a medium pan and bring to a boil over medium heat, stirring. Boil until the mixture is thickened and clear, about 2 minutes. Let the filling cool to room temperature.

Spread the cream cheese over the bottom of the cooled piecrust. Halve the remaining strawberries, then stir them into the cooled strawberry filling. Spread the strawberry filling over the cream cheese layer. Chill the pie until it is cold, at least 2 hours. Serve with lightly whipped cream.

Strawberry–Sour Cream Ice Cream serves 4

One of my favorite farm pictures from recent years is of my cousin Garth's son, Jonah, who is practically covered with sweet, melting ice cream running down his chin from the cone he's eating. The only thing better than ice cream is homemade ice cream. There's no need to cook this simple version before freezing: just blend everything together, pour into an ice-cream maker, and scoop into cones for a silky, tangy summer treat.

1 pound strawberries, trimmed, halved if large

¾ cup sugar

2 teaspoons lemon juice

Pinch of kosher salt

1 (16-ounce) container sour cream

1 cup heavy cream

In a large bowl, coarsely mash the strawberries with ¼ cup of the sugar, the lemon juice, and salt, using a potato masher.

Transfer half of the strawberry mixture to a blender and puree it with the sour cream, cream, and the remaining ½ cup sugar until smooth. Return the strawberry cream to the bowl with the remaining strawberries and stir to combine.

Freeze the mixture in an ice-cream maker, transfer to an airtight container, and freeze until firm.

My Grandmother's 1-2-3-4 Cake   serves 8 to 10

This 1-2-3-4 cake is a classic. The numbers dictate the ingredients: 1 cup butter, 2 cups sugar, 3 cups flour, 4 eggs. Just about everyone's grandmother made one, and there are many, many recipes for the cake on the Internet (although I have yet to find one with these exact proportions). The handwritten note on the back of the index card from my grandmother's recipe file reads, "P.S. This recipe was used for our wedding cake, Dec. 23, 1944," followed by a smiley face.

This is a simple cake to make, and it has great flavor. I like it by itself with coffee for breakfast or topped with the "Whipped Cream" Frosting (page 132), which is probably how my grandmother served it at her wedding.

2 sticks unsalted butter, at room temperature

2 cups sugar

1 teaspoon vanilla

4 large eggs, separated

3 cups sifted cake flour (sifted before measuring)

1 tablespoon baking powder

½ teaspoon kosher salt

1 cup whole milk

"Whipped Cream" Frosting (optional; page 132)

Preheat the oven to 375°F, with a rack in the middle. Butter and flour three 8-inch round cake pans or two 9-inch round cake pans.

Beat together the butter and sugar in a large bowl with an electric mixer until pale and fluffy, about 4 minutes. Add the vanilla and the egg yolks and beat until the batter is a few shades paler, 3 to 4 minutes.

Whisk together the flour, baking powder, and salt. Add half of the flour mixture to the butter mixture, mixing until it is just combined. Mix in the milk, then the remaining flour mixture.

Beat the egg whites until they just hold stiff peaks (but do not look dry), then gently fold them into the batter. Pour the batter into the cake pans, smoothing the tops.

Bake the cakes, rotating their positions in the oven for more even baking, until a tester or a toothpick comes out clean, 30 to 40 minutes.

Cool the cakes completely in the pans on racks. Frost the cake, if desired, or serve plain.

BY JULY, the first batch of unchecked weeds was as high as my shoulders. Back in June, I thought they might decide to top out at knee level, then at waist level, but clearly, these wild grasses and flowers thought they were oak trees. With an acute demonstration of nature's version of mind over matter, they were becoming exactly that. I had a garden of five-foot-tall oak trees. The weeds eagerly overtook the basil and the parsley. They created a jungle-like canopy covering the slow-growing tropical hot pepper plants. They threatened to choke out the chard. Something had to be done.

The only section of the garden that had not been overrun with weeds was the corn patch, the plot where we had researched and used biodynamic planting. There, we interspersed the corn with beans and summer squash. The practice—and it's an old one, used in Mexico since farming began—is called Three Sisters. Corn sucks nitrogen and nutrients from the soil, but beans replace them. The squash plants, low to the ground, fan out and block the sun, gaining the upper hand against weeds. It worked: all three plants produced lush, over abundant crops, and the weeds never grew past ankle height.

But the corn plot took up one tenth of the length of the garden. I spent the better part of a muggy July Friday carrying armfuls of wily grasses to the compost pile. Grass seed clung to my skin. I was sticky from sweat, itchy from weeds, and covered with dirt when I saw my cousin Leif's truck barreling up the lane.

"Hey, man," he called from the truck's cab, "I got a pig!"

I dropped my hoe where I stood, grabbed my T-shirt from where it hung on the fence post, and walked to Leif's idling pickup truck. "Let's go get 'im," he said. I hopped into the cab.

I had never cooked a whole pig before, and neither had Leif, but he had interviewed the local butcher, Frank Spera, at length. Frank, in his early seventies, was from the old school of butchering. He started with a whole animal and broke it down into familiar parts. Most modern butchers receive a box of identical and anonymous pieces, like shoulders, then cut them in a standardized fashion. Not Frank. He lent his personal spit to Leif, and his cooking instructions seemed simple. Rub the pig with salt. Place it on the spit. Use hardwood, not charcoal. Keep it covered and don't turn it. Cook it for nine hours. Frank wrapped a clear plastic tarp, the sort you might use for a painting drop cloth, around the pig's pink body and helped us carry it to the back of the truck. A hoof had poked its way through one end, a hairy chin through the other. We drove away and stopped off at a grocery store to buy bags of ice.

By the time we got to the store, the plastic, caught by the wind, had unfurled slightly, exposing the pig's midriff. Which is how we found ourselves explaining our plans for the roast to a police officer who had noticed the human-sized dead, naked body from across the parking lot. He walked with us back to the truck and peered in for a closer look before admitting that it sounded like a fun way to spend the weekend.

The next day, Saturday, was going to be an early one. We carried the pig to the cool, damp cellar of the farmhouse and packed it with ice. Leif said a few of his college classmates and friends would join us for the pig roast. I asked how many. "Oh, thirty or forty, I guess," he said. "But don't worry, I told them to bring tents." Around midnight, they started coming in waves. I went to bed, setting the alarm for 5:45.

By 6:00 everyone else was still asleep, and I was alone with an eight-foot spit, a pile of cherrywood, the low-hanging morning dew, and a 115-pound pig. I lit the fire in the spit, made some coffee, and waited for the wood to turn to coals. Sometime around 6:30, people started to rise, called to the day by the smell of brewing coffee and the gentle smoke of cherry.

By 7:00 three of Leif's friends had helped me skewer the pig and place it over the coals. We lowered the lid of the spit and started thinking about supper. Big Phil, one of Leif's friends, had plans to make a huge dish of mac 'n' cheese with herbs from the garden. Over the next nine hours, we fed the fire and checked on the pig. Friends and family pitched in with the never-ending list of farm chores, breaking every hour or so for beer. Kids ran through the yard carrying dripping ice-cream cones like Olympic torches, followed closely by a pack of dogs that were eager to clean cream-covered arms and chins.

By 4:00 p.m. we were starving and the pig was ready to eat. We lifted it, glistening and steaming, from the fire and placed it on a table. Ten of us swarmed the pig, picking off the tender bits with our hands, like pork-driven zombies. The cheeks and belly went first. Scorched fingers were a small price to pay for smoky, luscious, slow-roasted pork belly.

We sat at long tables set up in the yard and ate until the sun set. Big Phil's mac 'n' cheese was flecked with fresh thyme leaves and heady with homegrown garlic. Salads and vegetables from the garden offset the richness of the pork. We ate and ate and ate, and by the time we were ready to pack up the rest of the pig, we saw it could have fed crowds. We'd barely made a dent.

Whole Roast Pig   serves 60 to 80, with leftovers

It's difficult to find a recipe for cooking a whole pig. The best way to learn is 1) ask a butcher and 2) roast a whole pig. There are a few tricks I've picked up along the way that you'll probably find helpful if you've never roasted one before. The most noteworthy is that it is not necessary to turn the pig on the spit. Pigs are very fatty, and as they slowly cook, their fat melts down and through the meat — essentially, it's a self-basting animal. Instead, cover the grill (both the spit and the hole in the ground) and let the magic happen.

All the equipment can be gathered at a hardware store. Of course, if you can beg, steal, or borrow a spit, you'll save yourself the chore of digging a pit.

1 (100- to 115-pound) cleaned pig

1½ pounds kosher salt

Beer for basting (optional)

8 loaves bread (see page 197 or page 200)

Equipment you'll need: a shovel; 2 heavy-duty plastic garbage bags; 3 (4-foot-long) iron pipes and 1 couplet (to thread the pipes for the pig); tin wire; about 6 armloads of split hardwood; a large disposable aluminum tray; 1 (5-by-8-foot) sheet of corrugated tin roofing

Dig the pit: Dig a 4-by-6-by-4-foot-deep pit, trying to keep the sides and bottom as flat as possible for more

continued

even heat distribution. Dig a 6-inch-deep, 1-foot-long notch in the center of both of the short sides of the pit. This will take 3 to 6 hours, depending on how much help you have.

Cook the pig: Cut the garbage bags open to form sheets. Lay the plastic sheets on the ground. Place the pig on the plastic and rub it inside and out with the salt. Attach two of the pipes using the couplet. Skewer the pig onto the resulting 8-foot length of pipe by inserting the pipe through the anus, through the body cavity, and threading the pipe through the mouth or an incision in the throat. Tie the front legs together and the back legs together, near the hoofs, using the tin wire. Make an incision through one side of the rib cage with a sharp knife, cutting through to the cavity. Force the remaining pipe through the incision until it hits the far side of the cavity. Make another incision where the pipe has hit and feed the pipe through the other side of the rib cage so that it sticks out about 6 inches. Most of the pipe will remain on one side of the pig.

Arrange the hardwood along the long sides of the pit. Light a fire, and let the fire burn down to charcoal. This will take about 1 hour.

Lift the pig over the fire, letting the ends of the pipe spit rest in the notches in the pit. The pipe inserted through the rib cage will rest on the edge of the pit, preventing the pig from moving.

Brush any coals to the sides of the pit. Place the aluminum tray underneath the pig to catch any drippings. Cover the pit with the corrugated tin roofing. Cook, basting occasionally with beer, if desired, until the pig is cooked through, about 9 hours.

The ground retains an impressive amount of heat, so you'll need to add very little additional wood to the fire, if any, but check your pit every few hours to make sure it is still hot. This method of cooking produces very tender parts (belly, cheeks, shoulders) and juicy roasts (hind legs, loins, tenderloins).

Gently and carefully lift the pig from the pit and place it on a paper-lined serving table. Remove the pipes, then carve the pig into serving pieces. Serve the drippings with the bread.

Beer and Garlic Roast Pork   serves 8

This easy, supermarket-friendly recipe is written for all those pork lovers who aren't quite ready to commit to a whole pig. Use the butt end of the shoulder, which has more flavor than the leg end, and be sure to get one with a bone in it in case you feel like trying the Roast Pork Chili (opposite page); the bone adds a lot of flavor to the chili and to the roast. Chances are, you have most of the ingredients at home already, so all you'll need is the meat.

For the spice rub

2 tablespoons black peppercorns

2 tablespoons coriander seeds

1 bay leaf, broken into pieces

1 tablespoon finely grated orange zest

6 garlic cloves, finely chopped

3 tablespoons melted Master Fat (page 23) or extra-virgin olive oil

2 tablespoons kosher salt

For the pork

1 (6- to 8-pound) bone-in pork butt with skin

1 cup beer

1½ cups chicken stock or low-sodium broth

1 tablespoon unsalted butter or Master Fat (page 23)

1 tablespoon all-purpose flour

Make the spice rub: Grind the peppercorns, coriander seeds, and bay leaf in a spice grinder until they are finely ground. Stir the spices together with the orange zest, garlic, Master Fat, and salt.

Make the pork: Pierce the meat all over with the tip of a paring knife, making slits about 1 inch deep. Rub the pork all over with the spice rub and let it sit, loosely covered, in a flameproof roasting pan at room temperature for 1 hour.

Preheat the oven to 350°F.

Roast the pork, fat side up, until an instant-read thermometer registers 150°F, 1½ to 2 hours. Transfer the pork to a cutting board and let it rest for 30 minutes.

Pour off all but 1 tablespoon of the fat from the pan (add it to your Master Fat). Add the beer to the pan and bring it to a boil on the stovetop. Let the beer reduce by half, scraping up any browned bits from the pan, about 5 minutes. Add the stock and any juices from the cutting board to the pan and reduce to 1½ cups, about 5 minutes. Knead together the butter and the flour, then whisk the mixture into the sauce and boil, whisking, until the sauce is slightly thickened, about 2 minutes. Serve the pork with the sauce.

Roast Pork Chili   serves 8

There are two chili recipes in this book, and you should try them both. The venison chili on page 191 is Americanized and uses canned chipotles in adobo for heat. This recipe is based on a more traditional chili, like one you might find in Mexico, and relies on dried chiles for its depth of flavor. Feel free to switch the meats around (use pork instead of venison in the recipe on page 191, if you'd like) or even substitute beef chuck if that's more to your liking.

4 dried ancho chiles

4 dried guajillo chiles

1 pound ripe tomatoes or 1 (28- to 32-ounce) can whole tomatoes in juice

3½–4 pounds cooked bone-in pork shoulder, butt, and/or belly meat (or any combination thereof)

Kosher salt and black pepper

4 garlic cloves

2 teaspoons dried oregano

2 teaspoons distilled white vinegar

1 teaspoon ground cumin

6 black peppercorns

3 cloves

2 bay leaves

Accompaniments: corn tortillas, sliced radishes, diced white onion, crumbled queso fresco, salsa verde, chopped cilantro, thinly sliced iceberg lettuce

Slit the chiles lengthwise, then stem and seed them (leave the veins for heat). Heat a large heavy skillet (preferably cast-iron) over medium heat until hot, then toast the chiles in batches, opened flat, turning and pressing with tongs, until they are pliable and slightly changed in color, about 30 seconds per batch.

Transfer the chiles to a bowl and soak in hot water until they are softened, 15 to 25 minutes.

If using fresh tomatoes, cut a shallow X in the bottom of each tomato and blanch in simmering water for 20 seconds. Transfer the tomatoes with a slotted spoon to an ice bath to stop them from cooking. Peel the tomatoes. Coarsely chop the tomatoes, reserving their juice.

Preheat the oven to 350°F.

Cut the pork into large pieces and place in a 3-quart baking dish. Sprinkle all over with 1 teaspoon salt.

Drain the chiles, discarding the soaking water, and puree them in a blender with the tomatoes and reserved juice, ½ teaspoon salt, ½ teaspoon pepper, and the remaining ingredients until very smooth.

Pour the sauce over the meat, turning the meat to coat, then cover the dish tightly with a double layer of foil and braise in the oven until the meat is very tender, 2 to 3 hours. Remove from the oven and cool the meat in the liquid, uncovered, for 30 minutes.

Coarsely shred the meat, discarding any bones, then mix the meat into the braising liquid in the dish. Return the dish to the oven and cook, covered, until the sauce is simmering, another 30 minutes. Season the chili with salt and pepper to taste.

Serve the chili with warm tortillas and the other accompaniments.

Big Phil's Mac 'n' Cheese   serves 8

Phil Pukansky is a friend of my cousin Leif and has become a stalwart at the farm in recent years. It's always great to have him there because he pitches in every way he can, and there's a good reason for his nickname. Once, we were stacking six-foot logs to use later for firewood. I was holding one end, waiting for someone else to lift the other end so we could carry it together. Big Phil walked over and lifted the entire tree up by himself, with one arm. His willingness to help out doesn't end with log stacking: he's the first to volunteer in the kitchen, too. Big Phil loves food (it takes a lot of gas to keep such a powerful engine running). The first year we decided to roast a whole pig, Phil offered to make his famous mac 'n' cheese. Since then, he's made it every year, and it's always the first empty dish at the table.

1 head garlic

Olive oil

Kosher salt

1 pound elbow macaroni

4 slices bacon

3 large shallots, finely chopped

2 tablespoons all-purpose flour

4 cups heavy cream

2 teaspoons fresh thyme leaves

2 cups grated smoked cheddar cheese

1 cup grated Monterey Jack cheese

Black pepper

½ cup crumbled corn bread

2 tablespoons melted unsalted butter

Preheat the oven to 350°F. Butter a 13-by-9-inch baking dish.

Cut the top ½ inch off the head of garlic and discard. Place the trimmed head on a small piece of foil, drizzle with a little oil, and sprinkle with a pinch of salt. Wrap the garlic in the foil and roast for 45 minutes to 1 hour. Remove the foil and cool. (The garlic can be wrapped in plastic and refrigerated for up to a month.) Increase the oven heat to 400°F.

In a large pot of heavily salted boiling water, cook the pasta until it is al dente. Drain the pasta and reserve.

Cook the bacon in a large heavy skillet over medium heat until it is crisp, 6 to 8 minutes. Transfer the bacon to paper towels to drain, and pour off all but 2 tablespoons of the bacon fat (add it to your Master Fat).

Add the shallots to the skillet and cook, stirring occasionally, until they are browned, 6 to 8 minutes. Squeeze the garlic cloves out of their skins and into the skillet. Stir in the flour and cook, stirring, for 1 minute. Whisk in the cream and bring to a boil. Cook the sauce, whisking occasionally, until it is thickened and reduced by one third, about 10 minutes. Remove the skillet from the heat and stir in the thyme and both cheeses. Season the sauce with salt and pepper to taste.

Toss the pasta with the cheese sauce and transfer to the baking dish. Stir together the corn bread crumbs and melted butter, then sprinkle evenly over the mac 'n' cheese. Bake the mac 'n' cheese until the bread crumbs are golden and the mac 'n' cheese is bubbling, about 30 minutes. Let cool for 10 minutes, then crumble the bacon over the top and serve.

Grilled Corn with Chili-Cilantro Butter serves 12

Grilling corn in its husk is an easy way to cook the summer staple. The best part is that the cook isn't stuck shucking all the corn: you just throw the ears right on the grill in one layer and cover. The corn steams in its own husk and picks up a mild smokiness from the grill. When it comes time for dinner, everyone shucks his or her own and lathers the corn up with this simple butter that can be made up to a week in advance and refrigerated, wrapped in plastic. (This technique also works in a 425°F oven. Just place the ears of corn in their husks right on the oven rack.)

12 ears corn (with husks)

1 stick unsalted butter, at room temperature

4 teaspoons chili powder

2 garlic cloves, finely chopped

1 tablespoon honey

½ cup finely chopped cilantro

½ teaspoon kosher salt

½ teaspoon black pepper

Preheat the grill.

Place the corn ears in their husks over low-burning coals (or over low heat on a gas grill) and cover the grill. Cook the corn, turning occasionally, until it is tender, 35 to 45 minutes. Transfer the corn (still in the husks) to a serving platter.

Meanwhile, heat 2 tablespoons of the butter in a small heavy skillet over medium heat until it is melted. Stir in the chili powder and the garlic and cook, stirring constantly, until the garlic is golden and the chili powder is fragrant, less than 1 minute. Transfer the chili powder mixture to a food processor, then add the honey, cilantro, the remaining 6 tablespoons butter, salt, and pepper and pulse to combine. Transfer the chili-cilantro butter to a bowl and serve with the corn.

Turkey-Bacon Burgers serves 6 to 8

In my family, turkey burgers used to be met with an eye roll. After all, who wants turkey when you can have beef? But this recipe changes everyone's mind. Adding a little bacon to the mix makes all the difference. These are supermoist and so tasty you'll wonder why beef burgers are so popular.

1 garlic clove

4 ounces bacon

2 pounds ground turkey

1 medium onion, chopped

1½ teaspoons kosher salt

¾ teaspoon black pepper

Accompaniments: hamburger buns, ketchup, mustard, lettuce leaves, sliced tomato, sliced onion

With the motor running, drop the garlic clove into a food processor and finely chop. Add the bacon and pulse until it is finely chopped.

Gently mix the bacon and garlic into the ground turkey by hand, along with the onion, salt, and pepper.

Form the turkey mixture into 8 patties. Grill or fry the burgers until they are cooked through, 6 to 10 minutes.

Serve the burgers on buns with ketchup, mustard, lettuce, tomato, and onion.

Grilled Caesar Salad with Yogurt Dressing

serves 6

This salad becomes a favorite of everyone who tries it and gets an extra-summery taste from the few moments that the lettuce spends on the grill. Get your grill piping hot so the lettuce's outer leaves char before the rest of the head wilts. The goat's-milk yogurt in the dressing adds creaminess and acidity without a lot of fat, but feel free to use plain yogurt if you can't track down goat's-milk yogurt.

⅓ cup goat's-milk yogurt

2 tablespoons lemon juice

Kosher salt and black pepper

4 (½-inch-thick) slices country-style bread

2 tablespoons extra-virgin olive oil, plus more for drizzling

1 large garlic clove, halved

2 large heads romaine lettuce

¼ cup finely grated Parmigiano-Reggiano

Preheat the grill.

Whisk together the yogurt, lemon juice, ¾ teaspoon salt, and ½ teaspoon pepper.

Brush both sides of the bread slices with the oil, then grill the bread until it is toasted on both sides, 1 to 2 minutes. Rub both sides of the toasted bread with the cut side of the garlic clove.

Cut the romaine heads in half lengthwise, then grill them, turning once, until grill marks appear, about 2 minutes. Cut the romaine crosswise into 2-inch-wide strips and transfer to a large bowl.

Halve or quarter the toasts and add to the romaine along with the Parmesan.

Toss the salad with just enough dressing to coat, then drizzle with olive oil. Season with salt and pepper to taste and serve immediately.

Corn and Potato Salad serves 6

No regular potato salad, this simple combination is one of my most popular salads. It has its roots in a German-style potato salad, similar to those made by my family for generations, but this version incorporates more modern American flavors, like basil and cilantro. Instead of mayonnaise, there is an olive oil and vinegar dressing that brightly highlights the sweet corn and heady herbs. An outstanding addition to many, many picnics, it always gets completely eaten. It can be made a few hours ahead of time.

3 ears corn

2 pounds waxy potatoes, such as Yukon Gold or Red Bliss

Kosher salt

1 medium red onion

3 tablespoons apple cider vinegar

Black pepper

¼ cup extra-virgin olive oil

½ cup finely chopped fresh basil

½ cup finely chopped cilantro

Shuck the corn, then place the ears in a large pot with the potatoes. Add water to cover by 2 inches and 1 tablespoon salt and bring to a boil. Boil, covered, until the corn is tender, 2 to 4 minutes. Remove the corn and continue to boil the potatoes until they are very tender, 15 to 20 minutes.

While the potatoes cook, finely chop the onion and place it in a large bowl with the vinegar, 1 teaspoon salt, and ½ teaspoon pepper. Cut the kernels from the ears of corn and add to the onion in the bowl.

When the potatoes are very tender, drain them in a colander and add them to the bowl with the onion and corn. Add the oil and smash the potatoes coarsely with a masher. Let the potato salad come to room temperature, then add the herbs, season with salt and pepper to taste, and serve.

Smoked Cheddar and Jalapeño Corn Bread serves 6 to 8

Jalapeño and smoked cheddar make a unique and dense version of a classic American quick bread. It's best to use a cast-iron skillet for this one. If you don't have one already, this is your excuse to go out and get one. Cast-iron skillets are cheap, easy to maintain, great to cook with (I use them almost exclusively), and will last longer than you will. By the time you're gone, your skillet will be a family heirloom. Many of the cast-iron pans I use on a daily basis belonged to the cooks in my family generations ago.

½ stick unsalted butter

1¼ cups yellow cornmeal

¼ cup all-purpose flour

1 tablespoon sugar

1 teaspoon baking soda

¾ teaspoon kosher salt

½ teaspoon black pepper

2 large eggs

1¾ cups buttermilk

4 ounces smoked cheddar cheese, cut into cubes

1 jalapeño pepper, thinly sliced

Preheat the oven to 425°F.

Place the butter in a 10-inch cast-iron skillet and place the skillet in the oven for 10 minutes.

Whisk together the cornmeal, flour, sugar, baking soda, salt, and pepper. Whisk the eggs into the buttermilk in a large bowl, then whisk in the hot butter. Stir the cornmeal mixture into the buttermilk mixture, along with the cheese and jalapeño. Pour the batter into the hot skillet. Bake the corn bread until it is golden, 20 to 25 minutes. Turn the corn bread out of the skillet onto a rack to cool slightly. Serve it warm.

Molasses Raisin Walnut Cookies makes about 6 dozen

I remember the cookie jar in my grandmother's kitchen, brimming with freshly baked treats whenever we would visit. It was exciting to lift the lid and see what kind of cookie she had baked for us. This recipe of hers for supercrisp molasses cookies is one of my all-time favorites. The raisins and walnuts add texture and flavor, while the cookie itself is, well, just about perfect. I substitute butter for her shortening and skip the ½ cup of coconut that she often used.

1½ cups all-purpose flour

¾ teaspoon baking soda

¾ teaspoon kosher salt

1 stick unsalted butter, at room temperature

¾ cup sugar

1 large egg

¼ cup molasses

½ cup walnut pieces

½ cup raisins

Preheat the oven to 350°F, with a rack in the middle. Butter two baking sheets or line with parchment paper.

Whisk together the flour, baking soda, and salt.

In a large bowl, beat together the butter and sugar with an electric mixer until the butter looks pale and creamy, about 4 minutes. Beat in the egg and molasses. With a large spoon, stir in the flour mixture until it is just combined. Stir in the walnuts and raisins.

Place rounded teaspoonfuls of the dough on the baking sheets, spacing about 1 inch apart. Bake in batches until the cookies are evenly golden brown, 8 to 9 minutes. Let the cookies cool for a minute on the baking sheets before transferring them to a cooling rack. Store airtight.

Vanilla Bean–Mayonnaise Cupcakes with Chocolate Icing makes 16 cupcakes

As an ingredient in cake, mayonnaise makes perfect sense. It is made of eggs and oil, both common cake ingredients. Oil cakes, in general, tend to be very moist, and this one is no exception. I've added a vanilla bean, which brings deep flavor to the already moist and delicious cake. The glossy chocolate icing was a specialty of my grandmother.

For the cupcakes

1 cup whole milk

1 vanilla bean

2½ cups cake flour

1¾ teaspoons baking powder

½ teaspoon kosher salt

1 cup real mayonnaise

1 cup sugar

For the icing

2 tablespoons unsalted butter

2 (1-ounce) squares unsweetened chocolate

1 cup confectioners' sugar

3 tablespoons whole milk

½ teaspoon vanilla

¼ teaspoon kosher salt

Make the cupcakes: Preheat the oven to 350°F, with a rack in the middle. Line 16 cupcake cups with liners.

Add the milk to a small saucepan. Split the vanilla bean lengthwise and scrape the seeds into the milk with the side of a paring knife. Add the vanilla pod and bring the milk to a simmer, then remove from the heat. Cover the saucepan and let steep for 10 minutes. Discard the vanilla pod and cool the milk to room temperature.

Whisk together the flour, baking powder, and salt.

Beat together the mayonnaise and sugar in a large bowl until they are well combined. Add half the flour mixture, then beat in the milk. Beat in the remaining flour mixture. (The batter will be loose.) Divide the batter evenly among the cupcake liners.

Bake until the cupcakes are puffed and a toothpick inserted into the center comes out clean, about 20 minutes. Remove from the cupcake cups and cool on a rack.

Make the icing: Melt the butter in a medium saucepan over low heat. Add the chocolate and stir until it is melted. Remove from the heat and add the confectioners' sugar, milk, vanilla, and salt and beat with a wooden spoon until the icing is smooth and glossy. Let the icing cool slightly.

Spread the icing over the cooled cupcakes and serve.

Eating Between the Rows

Lamb's Quarters

FOR THE BETTER PART OF THE SUMMER, we eat wild greens alongside the lettuces, beet greens, and chard that we plant in the garden. We begin in the spring with sharp watercress and bittersweet dandelion, then move to lemony purslane and nutty lamb's-quarters by midsummer. Wild grapes, cherries, and wineberries are the sweetest treats after a long day of pulling nonedible weeds from the garden. By late August and early September, bright orange chanterelles speckle the woods like accidental drips from a late-summer sunset. The only trick is to learn which of nature's gifts are delicious and which are harmful. Much of this knowledge is common and has been passed down through generations. Some of it I've learned the hard way.

My mother tells a story from the late 1960s, just after she married my father. In it, my grandfather enters my grandmother's kitchen in early spring holding five squirrels in one hand and a bucket of weeds in the other. He says, "All right, Mary, here's your dinner." My mother still tells this story wincingly, but because of the squirrels, not the weeds, which were fresh young dandelion greens.

In my box of my grandmother's handwritten recipes is her version of a hot bacon dressing for dandelion greens. I make it every year. Simple country cooking, it includes egg, water, vinegar, sugar, and bacon—common ingredients that transform into the most delicious dressing. Tossed with baby dandelion greens, this dressing slightly wilts the greens. I do not have her recipe for squirrel.

Ramp Tagliatelle serves 4

Every spring people make a hullabaloo about ramps, the wild leeks that grow in the forests of the East Coast, for good reason: they're wonderful, with a garlic-heavy leek flavor and a subtle sweetness. I pickle the ramps, put them in just about everything we eat (they're particularly great in omelets), and give them away by the armload. This pasta is a simple way to highlight their flavor.

1 tablespoon extra-virgin olive oil

4 ounces ramps, white and pink parts finely chopped and greens cut into 1-inch pieces

Kosher salt

½ teaspoon black pepper

1 cup heavy cream

½ cup finely grated Parmigiano-Reggiano, plus more for sprinkling

8 ounces dried egg tagliatelle or fettuccine

Heat the oil in a deep heavy skillet (preferably cast-iron) over medium-high heat until it shimmers. Cook the white and pink parts of the ramps with ¾ teaspoon salt and the pepper, stirring occasionally, until they are golden, about 5 minutes. Add the cream and the ramp greens and boil until the sauce is slightly thickened, 2 to 3 minutes. Remove the skillet from the heat and stir in the Parmesan.

In a large pot of heavily salted boiling water, cook the pasta until it is al dente. Reserve 1 cup of the pasta-cooking water, then drain the pasta.

Add the pasta to the sauce in the skillet, along with ¼ cup of the cooking water, tossing to coat. Thin the sauce with more cooking water, if you prefer a looser sauce. Serve immediately, with additional cheese for sprinkling.

❊ RAMPS ❊

No COMBINATION OF GARLIC, SCALLION, and leek can ever quite match the primitive musk that fills your head when you chomp down on a ramp, or wild leek. It wasn't until I moved to New York City that I tasted my first ramps. If they grow wild in the woods of the farm, I've never found them. The irony that I needed to move away from the forest to discover them is not lost on me. But the ramps I ate from New York's Greenmarket and at restaurants around the city made me miss the country even more.

Ramps have cleverly made themselves scarce, thereby increasing demand. They have a very short season (only about six weeks in the spring), and they have the reputation for being uncultivable. The limited-season situation is true, and seemingly unavoidable, but the uncultivability is just a false rumor.

Ramps reproduce two ways. They flower and go to seed, like most plants. Those seeds then drop and make new plants. Ramps also reproduce by way of bulb offsets, which was the key to my patch.

I bought some at the farmers' market, making sure they came with roots, and planted them several years ago at the farm, and they took.

Before I planted the ramps, I removed the bottom ½ inch of bulb and left the roots attached. I stored them overnight, covered by room-temperature water. The next day, I planted them in the damp soil around an oak tree near the wild-watercress patch. I spent the next eleven months dreaming about the ramps and their heady scent.

The next spring, I checked the area where I had planted them. Sure enough, there they were. Every year I pick a few, and every year there are more ramps to enjoy. It has crossed my mind that the watercress patch, which we think of as wild, had once been cultivated, too. Someone, generations ago, might have placed the peppery cress at just the right spot in the woods, where it still lives. I hope the ramps last as long.

Seared Duck Breasts with Chanterelles serves 4

Whether you forage for your own mushrooms, as I do, or buy them from a trusted source (recommended for beginners), this recipe is an easy way to feature these totally delicious fungi. Fresh chanterelles have a seductive perfume that reminds me of apricots and black pepper, so it makes sense to add these ingredients to the sauce to help bring those flavors to the foreground. The sweetness from the apricot jam also balances the rich duck.

4 (6-ounce) Pekin duck breasts

Kosher salt and black pepper

1 teaspoon extra-virgin olive oil or Master Fat (page 23)

1 large shallot, finely chopped

1 pound fresh chanterelles, cut into 1-inch pieces

⅓ cup chicken stock or low-sodium broth

¼ cup apricot jam

1 tablespoon soy sauce

2 tablespoons unsalted butter

2 tablespoons finely chopped fresh flat-leaf parsley

Score the duck skin with a sharp knife, then sprinkle the breasts all over with ¾ teaspoon salt and ½ teaspoon pepper.

Heat the oil in a large heavy skillet over high heat until hot. Sear the duck, skin side down, until browned, about 4 minutes. Reduce the heat to medium and turn the duck over. Continue to cook for another 3 to 5 minutes or until the meat just begins to feel firm when pressed with a finger, for medium-rare. Transfer the duck to a cutting board to rest.

Add the shallot to the skillet and cook, stirring, until golden, about 3 minutes. Stir in the chanterelles, stock, jam, and soy sauce. Cover the skillet and cook until the mushrooms have softened, about 5 minutes. Uncover the skillet and boil until the liquid has reduced by about half and has started to thicken, about 3 minutes. Remove the skillet from the heat and whisk in the butter, then the parsley. Season the sauce with salt and pepper to taste.

Slice the duck breasts and serve with the mushrooms and sauce.

Shiitake-Stuffed Cornish Hens serves 8

One of my edible finds in the forest is a fungus called the honey mushroom (*Armillaria mellea*), because of its golden color. It has a deep woodsy flavor that is similar to shiitake (which is the mushroom you should use unless you are an expert mycologist). In this recipe, the water is cooked out of the mushrooms before they are stuffed inside small birds. You can use Cornish hens or poussins. The mushrooms absorb the birds' juices as they roast and, in turn, flavor the birds from the inside.

2 tablespoons extra-virgin olive oil or Master Fat (page 23)

1 large shallot, sliced

8 ounces fresh shiitake caps (or honey mushroom caps; see headnote), halved if large

Kosher salt and black pepper

2 tablespoons lemon juice

1 tablespoon finely chopped fresh flat-leaf parsley

4 (1¼- to 1½-pound) Cornish hens

½ cup dry vermouth

1 cup chicken stock or low-sodium broth

1 tablespoon unsalted butter

Preheat the oven to 450°F, with a rack in the middle.

Heat the oil in a large heavy skillet over medium-high heat until it shimmers. Add the shallot and sauté, stirring, until it is browned, about 4 minutes. Stir in the mushrooms, ½ teaspoon salt, and ¼ teaspoon pepper, then cover the skillet and cook for 3 minutes. Uncover the skillet and continue to cook, stirring occasionally, until all the liquid in the pan has evaporated, 4 to 6 minutes. Remove the skillet from the heat and stir in the lemon juice, parsley, and salt and pepper to taste.

Pat the hens dry and stuff the cavity of each with about ⅓ cup mushrooms. Place the hens in a large flameproof roasting pan and sprinkle them all over with 2 teaspoons salt and 1 teaspoon pepper. Tuck the wings underneath the bodies, then secure the legs together with a toothpick or tie with kitchen string.

Roast the hens for 20 minutes, then brush them with some pan drippings. Continue to roast, basting every 10 minutes, until the juices run clear when a thigh is pierced, 45 to 50 minutes total. Transfer the hens to a cutting board.

Straddle the roasting pan across two burners and add the vermouth. Bring to a boil, scraping up the browned bits. Add the stock and boil, stirring, until the sauce is slightly thickened and reduced to about 1 cup, 3 to 5 minutes. Remove the pan from the heat and whisk in the butter.

Scoop the mushrooms from the hens, then halve the hens. Serve with the mushrooms and sauce.

❈ MUSHROOMS ❈

By all accounts, foraging for mushrooms is a risky way to put food on the dinner table. Like race-car driving or BASE jumping, there's an inherent danger, even when you know what you're doing.

There are lots and lots of mushrooms that grow in the woods of the farm, and some of them are deadly. Many of them would make you only wish you were dead. And then, there are a few that are utterly delicious. The real problem, I've found, is that those delicious mushrooms very often have poisonous look-alikes. I thought about this one fall afternoon as I walked through the woods, hunting for something to eat with some fresh duck breasts I had in the fridge.

After only ten minutes, a scattering of fluorescent orange crossed the path. My heart jumped. Immediately I knew what they were: *Cantharellus cibarius*. Chanterelles are some of the meatiest and tastiest mushrooms you can find. But unfortunately, they've got some sinister doppelgangers.

The most toxic of the chanterelle's evil look-alikes is *Omphalotus olearius*, commonly known as the jack-o'-lantern mushroom. Here are some clues for identifying the jack-o'-lantern:

The mushrooms grow in clusters with a common base. They grow on rotting hardwood. They have gills. Here's the real giveaway: those gills glow in the dark—spooky.

I have found jack-o'-lantern mushrooms growing in the fall woods of the farm many times. One year, to test the glow-in-the-dark theory, I picked a large cluster and brought it back to the farmhouse. My cousin Dietrich and I waited until dark and placed the mushrooms on a chair in the living room. We took our seats on the couch and turned out the lights. It took only a few minutes for our eyes to adjust to the blackness, and as they did, the mushrooms started to become an iridescent green, appearing brighter and brighter as our eyes adjusted. After a short time, they glowed bright as neon. We didn't say a word until Dietrich broke the silence with a single, "Whoa." After that, we turned on the lights, threw out the mushrooms, and washed our hands. The jack-o'-lanterns probably wouldn't have killed us: they're in that second category, the kind that would have made us so sick, we would have wished for death.

This time, I was lucky, and that patch of bright orange mushrooms was, in fact, a group of chanterelles. This is how I could tell:

The chanterelles were growing singularly or in groups of two. They were growing from the dirt (not on hardwood), and instead of gills, they had what looked like forked veins. A forager's saying goes, "True chanterelles have false gills; false chanterelles have true gills."

I picked the chanterelles and kept walking. In another twenty minutes, my basket was full of two pounds of bright orange mushrooms that smelled distinctly of apricots and pepper. When I got back to the farmhouse, it was time for dinner.

Purslane Salad   serves 6

Lemony in flavor, with a crisp crunch, purslane makes a delicious base for this salad. If you're not adventurous enough to forage your own purslane, you can find it at some farmers' markets in the summer. It's also called pigweed, little hogweed, or verdolaga, depending on where you live.

3 tablespoons extra-virgin olive oil

1 tablespoon lemon juice

1 tablespoon finely chopped shallot

½ teaspoon kosher salt

¼ teaspoon black pepper

½ pint mixed cherry or small ripe tomatoes, halved or quartered if large

6 cups tender purslane leaves (about 1 pound)

4 cups mixed baby greens, such as arugula, parsley leaves, lamb's-quarters, spinach, or mizuna

Whisk the oil, lemon juice, shallot, salt, and pepper in a large bowl. Add the tomatoes, purslane, and mixed baby greens. Toss until coated and serve.

❈ PURSLANE AND SORREL ❈

IF YOU KEEP A GARDEN YEAR AFTER YEAR, you start to notice which plants take naturally to the soil and climate that are specific to your plot and which do not. Each little pocket of farmland has its own microclimate, and the plants respond to it.

I have the perfect microclimate for weeds.

I could spend hours each day weeding, and I would still have more weeds than vegetables. When I first started keeping this garden, I felt frustrated at how quickly and thickly the weeds grew. Now I just accept it. In fact, I even encourage them, because within the wild tangle, there are hidden gifts: purslane and sorrel.

My friends tease me that I feed them grass from the driveway as salad when they visit the farm in the summer. In fact, there's a lot of truth to that. The summer months are teeming with wild edible greens that, when tossed together with a simple lemon vinaigrette, become a satisfying summer salad. Purslane grows just about everywhere. I find it growing along the driveway of the farm.

I have found it growing in Brooklyn and in Central Park. It spreads over sidewalks and in alleyways all over the United States, and it grows especially well in my garden.

Sorrel is also a prolific squatter with a bright lemony tang. It sprouts up around the stone walls and in the yard near the farmhouse. It is often used in salads, but I love to play with the citrusy qualities of sorrel in sweet ways, too. I do my best to let people know its whereabouts so that they don't mow it down with a lawnmower. Inevitably, someone cuts it just when I'm ready to harvest it. On the off chance that I do get to pick the sorrel, I make a panna cotta featuring buttermilk (page 99).

Dandelion Greens Salad with Hot Bacon Dressing   serves 4 to 6

My grandmother tamed dandelion greens' bitterness with sugar, vinegar, and—what else?—warm, smoky bacon fat. The ingredients are staples of a Pennsylvania Dutch pantry—bacon, eggs, sugar, and vinegar—and they come together in a rich, warm dressing that barely wilts the greens. You can find dandelions at most farmers' markets and all over your backyard or garden. The trick is to pick them young—before the plants go to flower—when the greens are still very tender and less bitter.

4 slices bacon, chopped

1 large shallot, finely chopped

1 large egg

⅓ cup water

3 tablespoons distilled white vinegar

1 tablespoon sugar

Kosher salt

8 ounces young dandelion greens (about 14 cups)

Black pepper

Cook the bacon in a large heavy skillet over medium heat, stirring occasionally, until it is crisp, 6 to 8 minutes. Transfer the bacon to paper towels to drain, reserving the fat in the skillet.

Reduce the heat to low and add the shallot to the skillet. Cook, stirring occasionally, until softened, 4 to 6 minutes.

Whisk together the egg, water, and vinegar. Add the sugar and ¾ teaspoon salt to the skillet, then whisk in the egg mixture. Cook over low heat, whisking constantly, until the dressing is slightly thickened but not curdled, about 3 minutes.

Toss the dandelion greens with the hot dressing, then season with salt and pepper to taste. Serve sprinkled with the bacon.

Dandelion Greens with Garlic, Golden Raisins, and Pine Nuts serves 4

Young, tender dandelion greens are best in salad (see page 97), but once they grow up, you'll need to cook them. Flavorful counterpoints like raisins, garlic, and pine nuts complement the greens and moderate their bitterness.

12 ounces dandelion greens, cut into 2-inch pieces

¼ cup extra-virgin olive oil

⅓ cup pine nuts

¼ cup golden raisins, chopped

3 large garlic cloves, thinly sliced

1 teaspoon chopped pickled hot chile (page 153) or ¼ teaspoon dried red pepper flakes

Kosher salt and black pepper

2 teaspoons chile vinegar (page 153) or apple cider vinegar

Boil the dandelion greens in a pot of well-salted boiling water until they are crisp-tender and have lost their bitter taste, about 8 minutes. Drain the greens and, when cool enough to handle, press to extract as much liquid as possible.

Heat the oil in a large heavy skillet over medium heat until it shimmers. Add the pine nuts, raisins, garlic, chile, ½ teaspoon salt, and ¼ teaspoon pepper and cook until the pine nuts and garlic are golden, about 3 minutes.

Add the greens to the skillet and cook, stirring, until tender, 2 to 3 minutes. Stir in the vinegar, season with salt and pepper to taste, and serve.

Sorrel-Buttermilk Panna Cotta serves 8

Sorrel, which grows wild just about everywhere, is increasingly present at farmers' markets. I pick it from the fields at the farm, where it grows wild. It has a subtle, lemony flavor and often shows up in salads. Here, I've made it into a bright, lemony dessert. This panna cotta has just enough gelatin to hold its shape, so the result is a creamy, lemony pudding that melts in your mouth.

2¼ teaspoons unflavored gelatin

2 tablespoons cold water

6 cups sorrel (3½ ounces)

1½ cups buttermilk

1½ cups heavy cream

⅔ cup sugar

Pinch of kosher salt

Lightly sweetened whipped cream for serving

Lightly oil eight 3- to 4-ounce ramekins.

Sprinkle the gelatin over the water in a small bowl and let it stand for 1 minute to soften.

Puree the sorrel with the buttermilk in a blender until it is very smooth, about 1 minute. Strain the buttermilk mixture through a fine-mesh sieve into a medium bowl, pressing on the solids. Discard the solids.

Heat the cream with the sugar and salt in a small heavy saucepan over medium heat, stirring until the sugar has dissolved. Add the gelatin mixture and stir until dissolved. Pour the cream mixture into the buttermilk mixture, stir to combine, and divide among the ramekins. Cool completely, then cover the ramekins and refrigerate the panna cottas until they are set, at least 4 hours.

Serve the panna cottas with lightly sweetened whipped cream.

Sour Cherry Cordial makes about 1 quart

Wild cherries have a deep, sweet flavor, rich with almond and wild tartness. Soaking them in vodka macerates the fruit, and a little sugar syrup added at the end seals the deal. All winter I serve the sweet taste of midsummer to my most important guests. If you don't have wild cherries, use sour cherries instead.

2 cups wild or sour cherries

About 3 cups vodka

½ cup sugar

½ cup water

Place the cherries in a glass or plastic quart container with a lid. Muddle the cherries with a muddler or the handle of a wooden spoon until the cherries are all smashed. Add vodka to the container, filling it to the top. Cover the container and place it in the refrigerator for 3 weeks.

Strain the cherry cordial through a fine-mesh sieve.

Bring the sugar and water to a boil, stirring. Add the sugar syrup to the cordial, a little at a time, until it is sweet enough for your liking. (You'll want to use at least half of the sugar syrup.)

❋ WILD CHERRIES ❋

Life, no matter what they tell you, is not a bowl of cherries—but occasionally you'll get lucky enough to stumble upon a whole tree of them. I often take a long walk through the cool of the woods as a break from the sun's glare. Of course, I always keep my eyes peeled for dinner.

On one of my walks, I had my eyes on the ground, waiting for something, anything, to jump out and cry, "Eat me!" All of a sudden, there it was: a tiny fruit the size of a pebble, shiny and almost black in color, attached to a long, skinny stem. It had been half eaten. The birds knew. This little fruit was a wild cherry. I cast my eyes skyward. There, dangling about twelve feet above me, hung constellations of perfectly ripe fruit.

Half an hour later, I was teetering atop an old apple-picking ladder that I'd found tucked in the corner in the wagon shed, plucking one tiny cherry at a time. I popped one in my mouth. It burst with sweetness and juice but was mostly pit, not the kind of cherry for making a pie.

It's a nice way to spend an afternoon, plucking little wild cherries, but a full hour later, I had only about two cups' worth. I packed the ladder away and washed the fruit.

I put the cherries in a plastic quart container and mashed them with a muddler. Their juice was bloodred, and the little splashes that escaped the container stained the chopping block crimson. I poured vodka on top of the cherries, pits and all, and kept it covered for a week.

When I peeled back the lid, I was hit square in the face with stone-fruit perfume, an olfactory cherry bomb. The alcohol macerated the fruit, extracting its sweet-tart essence. I strained the elixir and added sugar syrup to taste.

There's a lesson here: When you're handed a wild cherry tree, make cherry cordial.

Homemade Yogurt with Wineberries in Honey Syrup serves 4

A wild relative of the raspberry, wineberries grow in the woods and along the roads near the farm and almost everywhere else in the Northeast. Originally from northern Asia, they were introduced to this country to be crossbred with raspberries, but they escaped captivity and took well to the climate and soil. Some people say they are an invasive species. I call them a treat. The berries, which look like polished rubies and taste like raspberry wine, ripen in late July. They are great eaten right off the bush, on vanilla ice cream, or for breakfast or dessert with some homemade yogurt. If there are no wineberries where you live, use raspberries instead.

For the yogurt

1¾ cups whole milk

¼ cup heavy cream

2 tablespoons whole-milk yogurt

For the berries

¼ cup honey

¼ cup water

Pinch of kosher salt

1 cup wineberries or raspberries

Make the yogurt: Heat the milk and cream to 180°F in a saucepan. Cool the milk mixture to 110°F, then stir in the yogurt. Transfer the milk mixture to a pint jar and place the jar in a warm water bath. Replace the water with warm water (100° to 105°F) as it cools. Let the yogurt incubate at room temperature until thickened, replacing the water as necessary, 5 to 7 hours. Pour the yogurt into a paper-towel-lined sieve set over a bowl. Cover the surface of the yogurt with plastic wrap and refrigerate overnight.

Make the berries: Heat the honey and the water with the salt, stirring until the honey is dissolved.

Pour the syrup over the wineberries in a bowl and let macerate for 10 minutes. Serve the yogurt topped with the berries and syrup.

Blueberry Belle Crunch   serves 6 to 8

An old family favorite, this crumble recipe has been passed down to me from my Aunt Janet, who learned it from my grandmother. Honestly, I have no idea why it has such a funny title, but it doesn't matter. It's so easy to throw together that no matter what you call it, you'll be more than happy with the result. It's especially wonderful served warm with a scoop of vanilla ice cream on the side.

For the berries

12 ounces fresh blueberries

½ cup sugar

2 tablespoons all-purpose flour

2 tablespoons lemon juice

¼ teaspoon kosher salt

For the crunch

¾ cup all-purpose flour

½ cup quick-cooking oats

½ cup light or dark brown sugar

½ teaspoon vanilla

½ teaspoon kosher salt

1 stick unsalted butter, cut into cubes

Ice cream for serving

Preheat the oven to 375°F, with a rack in the middle. Generously butter a 9-inch pie plate.

Make the berries: Toss the blueberries with the sugar, flour, lemon juice, and salt. Transfer the berries to the pie plate.

Make the crunch: Stir together the flour, oats, brown sugar, vanilla, and salt. Blend in the butter with your hands until well combined. Crumble the topping over the berries in large clumps.

Bake the crunch until the berries are bubbling and the crunch is set and browned in places, 25 to 35 minutes.

Let the crunch cool slightly before serving. Serve with ice cream.

THE POND IS ALWAYS around fifty degrees, so on any day but the hottest, it is too cold to swim in. The bottom of the pond is mucky and silty. The best word to describe the way it feels when you stand there, sinking up to your calves in muck, is "icky." There are at least a few snapping turtles, the size of small dinosaurs, that swim through the muddy water. Oh, and there are little leeches living in the mud that will attach themselves to your legs as soon as you enter the water. But once a year, there is an August day so hot that I jump eagerly into the algae-filled, spring-fed waters. It's worth it every time.

I could tell when I woke up that morning that it was going to be a pond day. I sat on the steps to the porch and tied my boots with double knots. The 7:00 a.m. sun beat down hard, drawing the day's first beads of sweat to my forehead. There is a certain scent to deep summer mornings: rich and dry, like the smell of baseboard heat.

I ate three cherry tomatoes from the plant for breakfast. Their skins were hot, and they burst in my mouth, sending forth a rush of sweet seeds and flesh, still cool from the night. The lettuces and beet greens held a full salute. By the day's end, they would wilt and faint where they stood. That evening, we would need to water.

All morning we worked in the sun, and by early afternoon, the grass had been mowed, the weeds had been pulled, and the tomatoes and Swiss chard had been picked. I walked into the corn and zucchini patch. The shade of the cornstalks was no relief from the sun. I bent down to search for squash. Close to the ground, the large zucchini leaves had trapped moisture. It felt like a steam sauna. That day our sweat poured into the soil in such volume that I wondered if perhaps the vegetables would be seasoned with it. The pond was looking really good.

In another ten minutes, six of us were removing our boots and shirts. We jumped off the rickety dock wearing only our underwear. When my body hit the water, I lost my breath. I let myself hang there, just beneath the surface, for a full ten seconds. My arms tingled with the shock of the cold. A giant splash just to my left brought me bobbing back to the heat of the air. It was Leif. He'd brought a plastic bag of beer cans and tied them to the dock so they would chill in the cold water without sinking into the muck. Dave cracked open a few and passed them around. We all floated there in the cool relief of the mineral-rich water and drank our beers. The dogs swam back and forth over the length of the pond, lifeguarding and threatening to save anyone who let go of the dock, until Cecily called to us from the porch. Lunch was ready. We walked up to the house, dripping. My skin felt cold. We took turns spraying our legs with the hose on full stream to knock the tiny leeches away.

Cecily had made BLTs for lunch using arugula in addition to lettuce. She'd plucked a few ripe tomatoes and sliced them thickly, then sprinkled them with cracked black pepper. The sandwiches were creamy with mayo and arugula pesto and crisp with salty bacon. We were hungry. I ate two BLTs and pulled on my jeans. In the heat of the early afternoon, I was already dry.

The walls of the farmhouse are three feet thick, made of stone and held together with some sort of rudimentary cement of horsehair, mud, and whatever else was available at the time. The stone absorbs heat all summer, cooling the house, and holds in the heat in winter, keeping the temperature above freezing. But this day, the stones had met their match. The summer sun was so intense that the stones had become saturated with heat, enough to last through January.

A few friends decided to take a trip in the air-conditioned car to the nearby Mennonite dairy farm to see if they could find some good cheeses. I lay down in the shade of a black walnut tree and fell asleep, sweating as I dreamed.

Some hours later, I woke up to the sound of a car zooming up the lane. They had found the dairy farm and had stopped at the distributor to buy beer and bask in the cool of the walk-in refrigerator. I squinted and worked myself to my feet.

The dairy farm proved to be a sanctuary of cheese. They had stocked up on cheddars and cheese curds, but one cheese stood out. It was a gooey spread made from cheddar, sour cream, and bits of bacon, whipped together until it was airy. I ran a finger through it and tasted. It would be easy to make, and I was already imagining ways to use it, like on a pizza with cherry tomatoes and arugula. That gave me an idea for dinner. It was too hot to cook inside but a perfect day to grill. We lit the fire, cracked open the cold beers, and started talking about pizza.

Grilling pizza can be tricky, and the first batch of dough stuck to me as I tried to lift it onto the grill. I walked into the farmhouse kitchen with a burnt arm and burnt dough, feeling defeated. My friend Michelli, a professional cook and food stylist, shook her head and took over.

She stretched the dough into a rectangle, floured it well, and placed it on a cookie sheet. Then, without any trouble at all, she slid the dough from the cookie sheet right onto the hot grill. The dough was crispy and charred in just the right places. When we sat down to dinner, we toasted the Mennonite cheese spread that had melted into a sauce for one of our pizzas and Michelli, for saving our meal.

Chilled Corn Soup
with Red Pepper Relish serves 6 to 8

A small cup of corn chowder is a great way to kick off any summertime feast. This recipe is a good use of a lot of corn. The cobs are included in the broth, and they add a surprising depth of flavor. Of course, you can serve this soup hot off the stove, but in the summer, I love the cool, silky texture when it is served cold. The sweetness of the corn comes through and helps make this chowder both satisfying and refreshing. If you happen to have extra corncobs from, say, Silky Savory Summer Sour Cream Flan (page 117) or Corn and Potato Salad (page 82), feel free to toss them in the pot for a little extra flavor.

For the soup

6 ears corn

2 tablespoons Master Fat (page 23) or extra-virgin olive oil

1 sweet onion, chopped

1 garlic clove, minced

3 cups water

3 cups whole milk

Kosher salt

Black pepper

For the relish

1 red bell pepper

⅓ cup red wine vinegar

1 large shallot, thinly sliced

½ teaspoon kosher salt

2 tablespoons finely chopped fresh dill

1 tablespoon extra-virgin olive oil

¼ teaspoon black pepper

Make the soup: Cut the kernels from the cobs, then cut the cobs in half crosswise. Heat the fat in a heavy pot over medium heat until it shimmers. Add the onion and garlic and cook, stirring occasionally, until the onion is softened, but not browned, 4 to 5 minutes. Stir in the water, milk, corn kernels and cobs, and 1¾ teaspoons salt and bring to a simmer. Cook until the corn kernels are very tender, 8 to 10 minutes. Discard the cobs. Puree the soup in a blender in batches (be careful blending hot liquids), then chill the soup in the refrigerator until it is cold. Season the soup with salt and pepper to taste.

Make the relish: Roast the bell pepper under the broiler or on the grill, turning occasionally, until the skin is charred and blistered. Place the pepper in a bowl and cover the bowl so the pepper steams. When the pepper is cool enough to handle, peel and chop, discarding the skin, seeds, stem, and veins.

Bring the vinegar to a boil in a small saucepan. Stir in the shallot and ¼ teaspoon of the salt. Remove the saucepan from the heat and let stand for 10 minutes. Drain the shallot, then toss it with the bell pepper, dill, oil, pepper and the remaining ¼ teaspoon salt.

Serve the soup in cups, topped with the red pepper relish.

Zucchini Pizza   serves 4 to 6

Pretty much everything is better when you put it on pizza, and the first zucchini of the summer is no exception. This pie is unusual in that it doesn't have a sauce, but the zucchini softens into the crisp, charred crust, and you're left only wanting one thing: more. The flavors of this pizza are clean, simple, irresistible.

2 pounds zucchini

2 teaspoons kosher salt

6 tablespoons extra-virgin olive oil

1½ pounds Pizza Dough (page 113)

½ cup finely grated Parmigiano-Reggiano

1 garlic clove, finely chopped

1 hot red chile, finely chopped

Black pepper

Trim the zucchini, then thinly shave using an adjustable slicer or a sharp knife. Toss the zucchini with the salt, then let sit in a sieve set over a bowl at room temperature for 30 minutes. Rinse the zucchini, then squeeze to remove as much liquid as possible.

Preheat the oven to 500°F, with a rack in the lowest position. If you have a pizza stone, place it on the rack.

Coat a large baking sheet with 2 tablespoons of the oil, then turn the dough over on the pan to coat it with oil. Pull and stretch the dough to fit the pan, leaving the center thinner and the edges thicker. Let the dough rest for 10 minutes.

Bake the dough, turning the pan occasionally, until it is mostly browned and crispy, 12 to 15 minutes.

Sprinkle half the Parmesan evenly over the dough. Scatter the zucchini, garlic, and chile evenly over the dough. Sprinkle the remaining Parmesan evenly over the zucchini, drizzle with the remaining 4 tablespoons oil, and season with pepper to taste.

Return the pan to the oven and continue to bake the pizza until the edges of the zucchini are browned, 8 to 12 minutes. Serve.

Grilled BLT Pizza serves 4 to 6

This recipe was inspired by an amazing bacon-cheddar spread made at a nearby Mennonite farm. The flavors in the spread (cheddar, sour cream, bacon) are not what you'd think of as typical pizza material, but as a base for this dish, it's just about perfect. The ripe cherry tomatoes bubble and burst as they cook, and the peppery arugula wilts ever so slightly when it's added at the very end. If you can't grill the pizza, you can bake it in the oven (see the variation).

2 slices bacon

4 ounces sharp white cheddar cheese

¼ cup sour cream

¼ teaspoon kosher salt

½ teaspoon black pepper

1½ pounds Pizza Dough (page 113)

1 pint cherry tomatoes, halved

2 cups arugula

¼ cup finely grated Parmigiano-Reggiano

2 tablespoons extra-virgin olive oil

Pulse the bacon, cheddar, sour cream, salt, and pepper in a food processor until smooth.

Preheat the grill. If you are using charcoal, spread the coals evenly once they are hot, for more even cooking. Generously flour a baking sheet.

Flour your work surface and your hands. Stretch the dough to form a 12-by-17-inch rectangle, then place it on the baking sheet and let the dough rest for 10 minutes.

When you are ready to grill, gently slide the dough from the baking sheet onto the grill rack. Cover the grill and cook until the dough is set and grill marks appear, 2 to 6 minutes, depending on the heat of your grill. Transfer the dough back to the baking sheet, grilled side up.

Spread the bacon-cheese mixture evenly over the dough. Scatter the tomatoes evenly over the dough. Slide the pizza back onto the grill rack, then cover the grill. Cook the pizza until the bottom is charred and the dough is cooked through, 3 to 8 minutes.

Before serving, top the pizza with the arugula, sprinkle with the Parmesan, and drizzle with the oil.

Oven Variation

Preheat the oven to 500°F, with a rack in the lowest position. If you have a pizza stone, place it on the rack. Spread 2 tablespoons olive oil on a large baking sheet, then turn the dough over on the pan to coat it with oil.

Pull and stretch the dough to fill the pan, leaving the center thinner and the edges thicker. Let the dough rest for 10 minutes.

continued

Bake the dough, turning the pan occasionally, until it is set and some brown spots appear, 12 to 15 minutes. Remove the dough from the oven and spread the bacon-cheese mixture evenly over the dough. Scatter the tomatoes evenly over the dough.

Return the pizza to the oven and continue to cook until the dough is cooked through and the tomatoes just start to wilt, 8 to 12 minutes. Before serving, top the pizza with the arugula, sprinkle with the Parmesan, and drizzle with the oil.

Pizza Dough   makes 1½ pounds dough or one 12-by-17-inch pizza crust

This is a versatile recipe for any kitchen, so keep this one in heavy rotation. Once the dough rises for an hour, it can be punched down and frozen for later use. When you're ready to use it, let the dough come to room temperature and continue with the pizza recipe. Using bread flour instead of all-purpose produces a slightly chewier, crispier crust.

1 teaspoon active dry yeast

1 cup warm water

3 cups bread flour or all-purpose flour (see headnote)

3 tablespoons extra-virgin olive oil

2 teaspoons kosher salt

Stir together the yeast and water until the yeast is dissolved.

To mix in a stand mixer: Add the flour, yeast mixture, oil, and salt to the bowl of the mixer and beat with the paddle attachment on low speed until combined. Increase the speed and knead the dough until it pulls away from the edges of the bowl. Scrape the dough into a ball and let it rest in the bowl, covered with a towel, at room temperature until it doubles in size, about 1 hour in a warm room.

To mix by hand: Stir the ingredients together in a large bowl until they are combined, then transfer the dough to a flourless work surface. Knead the dough until it becomes elastic and pulls off the work surface. (The dough will still be sticky.) Oil the bowl, then shape the dough into a ball and place it back in the bowl, turning the dough to coat with oil. Cover the bowl with a towel and let the dough rest at room temperature until it doubles in size, about 1 hour in a warm room.

Swiss Chard and Fresh Ricotta Pizza serves 6

When I told Zanne Stewart, my former editor at *Gourmet*, about this book, she expressed relief that she'd finally have enough recipes to use up all of the Swiss chard she gets from her CSA, her weekly share of farm produce. This recipe uses two whole bunches of the stuff on an unlikely (but well-loved) canvas. The inspiration came from the venerable spinach pies of the many New York pizza shops I have frequented. Don't be shy with the dollops of ricotta: they add a wonderful milkiness to the earthy greens.

2 bunches Swiss chard
(1½ pounds)

6 slices bacon, chopped

4 tablespoons extra-virgin olive oil

5 garlic cloves, thinly sliced

¼ teaspoon dried red pepper flakes

Kosher salt and black pepper

1½ pounds Pizza Dough (page 113)

1½ cups fresh ricotta (see page 22)

¼ cup chopped brined capers

2 teaspoons finely grated lemon zest

Separate the Swiss chard leaves and stems. Tear the leaves into large pieces and chop the stems.

Cook the bacon with 2 tablespoons of the oil in a large heavy skillet over medium heat, turning occasionally, until the bacon just starts to brown, 4 to 5 minutes. Add the garlic, pepper flakes, 1 teaspoon salt, and ½ teaspoon pepper and cook, stirring occasionally, until the garlic is golden, 1 to 2 minutes. Add the chard stems and increase the heat to medium-high. Sauté, stirring occasionally, until the stems are almost tender, about 4 minutes. Add the leaves and sauté, stirring occasionally, until the leaves are wilted, 5 to 6 minutes. Remove the skillet from the heat and season with salt and pepper to taste.

Preheat the oven to 500°F, with a rack in the lowest position. If you have a pizza stone, place it on the rack.

Coat a large baking sheet with the remaining 2 tablespoons oil, then turn the dough over on the pan to coat it with oil. Pull and stretch the dough to fit the pan, leaving the center thinner and the edges thicker. Let the dough rest for 10 minutes.

Bake the dough, turning the pan occasionally, until it is mostly browned and crispy, 12 to 15 minutes.

Remove the pan from the oven, then spread the Swiss chard mixture evenly over the dough. Dollop the ricotta over the chard, then sprinkle evenly with the capers and lemon zest.

Return the pan to the oven and continue to bake the pizza until the ricotta starts to brown, 8 to 12 minutes. Serve.

Ceci's BLT makes 4 sandwiches

Long before we started the farm garden, my sister Cecily grew her own tomato plants in the window of her Philadelphia apartment. Ceci's BLT provides a stage for her ripe tomatoes to shine. She meticulously toasts the bread, makes a flavorful arugula-basil pesto, and adds just enough garlic to the mayonnaise to bring intrigue without overpowering the other flavors. The bacon she uses is extra-smoky, and the lettuce is buttery soft, with cool, crunchy ribs. And the tomatoes? She handpicks them just for this sandwich, slices them as thick as steaks, and stacks them in a tower between the golden toasted bread slices. One bite and you'll know why you decided to plant your own tomatoes this year; all that work is instantly worth it.

8 slices bacon

About 2 tablespoons extra-virgin olive oil

2 cups arugula

1 cup fresh basil leaves

1/3 cup finely grated Parmigiano-Reggiano

1/3 cup pecans, toasted

Kosher salt and black pepper

1 small garlic clove

1/4 cup mayonnaise

8 slices sourdough Pullman or hearty white bread, toasted

2–3 beefsteak tomatoes

4 large butter lettuce leaves

Cook the bacon in a large heavy skillet (preferably cast-iron) over medium heat, turning occasionally, until crisp. Transfer the bacon to paper towels to drain. Pour the fat from the skillet into a glass measuring cup and let it cool to room temperature. Add enough olive oil to bring the level to 1/4 cup.

Place the arugula, basil, Parmesan, pecans, and 1/4 teaspoon each salt and pepper in a food processor. With the motor running, pour the fat-oil mixture into the pesto and process until blended.

Mash the garlic to a paste with a pinch of salt, then stir it into the mayonnaise.

Spread some of the pesto on 4 slices of toast. Spread the mayonnaise on the remaining 4 slices of toast. Slice the tomatoes 1/2 inch thick. Layer the tomatoes on the pesto-topped toast and sprinkle with a pinch of salt and pepper. Top with the bacon, lettuce, and the remaining toasts, mayonnaise side down, and serve.

Corn and Parmesan Pesto with Tagliatelle serves 4 to 6

This recipe takes a summer staple, corn, and blends it to make a terrific and unexpected base for this sweet and nutty pesto. Instead of blending those gorgeous basil leaves into oblivion, use them for garnish.

3 tablespoons plus ⅓ cup extra-virgin olive oil

4 cups fresh corn kernels (cut from about 6 large ears)

1 medium onion, chopped

1 large garlic clove, minced

Kosher salt and black pepper

½ cup finely grated Parmigiano-Reggiano, plus more for serving

⅓ cup pine nuts, toasted

8 ounces tagliatelle or fettuccine

¾ cup coarsely torn fresh basil leaves

Heat 3 tablespoons of the oil in a large heavy skillet over medium-high heat until it shimmers. Add the corn, onion, garlic, 1¼ teaspoons salt, and ¾ teaspoon pepper and sauté until the corn is just tender but not brown, about 4 minutes. Transfer 1½ cups of the corn kernels to a small bowl. Scrape the remaining corn mixture into a food processor. Add the Parmesan and pine nuts. With the machine running, add the remaining ⅓ cup olive oil and blend until the pesto is almost smooth.

Cook the pasta in a large pot of heavily salted boiling water until al dente. Reserve 1½ cups of the pasta-cooking water, then drain the pasta. Return the pasta to the pot. Add the corn pesto, the reserved corn kernels, and ½ cup of the basil leaves. Toss the pasta over medium heat until warmed through, adding the reserved pasta-cooking water to thin to the desired consistency, 2 to 3 minutes. Season the pasta to taste with salt and pepper.

Transfer the pasta to a large shallow bowl. Sprinkle with the remaining ¼ cup basil leaves. Serve the pasta with additional Parmesan.

Silky Savory Summer Sour Cream Flan serves 6

Zucchini and corn grow together, so it only makes sense that they go so well together. Here, their natural sweetness is balanced by the slight tang of the sour cream in a decadent egg custard that is similar to a crustless quiche. This is a great lunch or light dinner when paired with a simple salad and a glass of crisp white wine. It also makes for a stellar brunch dish that is both satisfying and summery.

2 medium zucchini

3 ears corn

1 medium onion, chopped

2 garlic cloves, minced

2 tablespoons extra-virgin olive oil

1½ teaspoons kosher salt

½ teaspoon black pepper

7 large eggs

1 cup sour cream

¼ cup finely grated Parmigiano-Reggiano

6 squash flowers (optional)

Halve the zucchini lengthwise and cut into ¼-inch slices. Cut the kernels from the corncobs.

Preheat the oven to 350°F, with a rack in the middle.

Cook the onion and garlic in the oil in a 10-inch cast-iron or ovenproof nonstick skillet over medium-high heat until they just start to brown, about 6 minutes. Add the zucchini and corn, along with ¾ teaspoon of the salt and ¼ teaspoon of the pepper. Cook, stirring occasionally, until the zucchini is very soft, about 10 minutes.

Meanwhile, whisk together the eggs, sour cream, Parmesan, the remaining ¾ teaspoon salt, and the remaining ¼ teaspoon pepper. Pour the egg mixture evenly over the vegetables and remove the skillet from the heat. Tear the squash flowers (if using) and place them evenly over the custard.

Transfer the skillet to the oven and bake until the flan is just set in the center, 20 to 30 minutes.

Remove the flan from the oven and let it stand for 5 minutes before serving. It will be slightly loose, but it will hold together when cut into slices.

Summer Chicken 'n' Biscuit Pie

Summer Chicken 'n' Biscuit Pie serves 6 to 8

This recipe is the one that might just bring the potpie back as a modern dinnertime staple. A light biscuit crust soaks up the tomato juices as the pie bakes (see the photo on pages 118–119). Originally, I made this dish to use up some leftover chicken salad and corn, and it ended up being everyone's favorite. Roast the chicken yourself or buy a rotisserie chicken at the store.

For the crust

4 cups all-purpose flour

1½ teaspoons baking powder

½ teaspoon baking soda

1 stick unsalted butter, cut into cubes

½ cup shortening

¾ teaspoon kosher salt

1½ cups buttermilk

For the filling

3 cups shredded roast (or poached) chicken

½ cup mayonnaise

4 ears corn

2 large tomatoes

¼ cup finely chopped fresh herbs (dill, basil, oregano, cilantro)

1 tablespoon apple cider vinegar

2 tablespoons fine cornmeal

¾ teaspoon kosher salt

¾ teaspoon black pepper

Make the crust: Work together the flour, baking powder, baking soda, butter, shortening, and salt with your hands in a large bowl until the dough is combined, with some small lumps of butter remaining. Add the buttermilk and stir with your hands, kneading gently to combine the dough (the dough is wet and sticky, which makes for a fluffier biscuit). Divide the dough in half. Wrap each half in plastic and chill for 1 hour.

Meanwhile, make the filling: Stir the chicken together with the mayonnaise. Cut the corn kernels from the cobs and place the kernels in another bowl. Chop the tomatoes and toss them with the corn and the remaining ingredients.

Preheat the oven to 425°F, with a rack in the middle.

Roll one half of the dough between two sheets of plastic wrap into an 11-inch round. Remove the top layer of plastic wrap, then transfer the dough, using the plastic wrap to guide the dough, to a 9-inch pie plate (dough side down). Remove the plastic wrap. Roll the remaining dough out the same way and keep it ready.

Fill the pie with the chicken mixture, then top the chicken with the corn and tomato mixture.

Cover the filling with the remaining biscuit dough the way you did before. Remove the plastic wrap and pinch the edges of the dough together by lifting the bottom crust up and over the top crust. Cut three steam vents in the top crust.

Bake the pie until the crust is golden brown all over, 30 to 45 minutes. Let the pie stand for 15 minutes before serving.

Brick Chicken with Corn and Basil Salad   serves 4 to 6

This technique (one I stole from Tuscan cooking) produces some of the juiciest chicken, with ultracrispy skin. The preheated bricks help the chicken cook faster, saving as much of its juices as possible. My young cousins love wrapping the bricks in foil and placing them on the grill to preheat. The raw corn salad is best with only the freshest, sweetest corn and the greenest basil and adds lightness to the dish, balancing the smoky flavor of the chicken.

For the chicken

1 (3½-pound) chicken

1 teaspoon finely grated orange zest

½ cup fresh orange juice

¼ cup extra-virgin olive oil

2 large scallions, finely chopped

1 garlic clove, smashed

1 teaspoon cumin seeds

1 teaspoon apple cider vinegar

1½ teaspoons kosher salt

1 teaspoon black pepper

For the corn salad

4 ears very fresh corn

1 tablespoon finely chopped shallot

2 tablespoons extra-virgin olive oil

1 tablespoon lime juice

¼ cup chopped fresh basil

1 teaspoon kosher salt

½ teaspoon black pepper

Make the chicken: Remove the backbone of the chicken by cutting down along both sides with kitchen shears. Flatten the chicken by pressing down on the breast. Stir together the orange zest, juice, oil, scallions, garlic, cumin seeds, vinegar, salt, and pepper. Place the chicken in a large sealable plastic bag, then pour the marinade over the chicken and seal the bag. Marinate the chicken, chilled, turning the bag once or twice, for at least 4 hours.

Wrap two bricks with aluminum foil. Preheat the grill, covered, with the bricks on the grill rack, for at least 20 minutes.

Remove the chicken from the marinade. Oil the grill rack. Place the chicken, skin side down, on the grill rack over the coals, then place the bricks on top of the chicken. Grill the chicken, covered, until the skin is crisp and browned, about 15 minutes. Remove the bricks and flip the chicken over. Place the bricks back on top of the chicken. Continue to grill until the chicken is cooked through, 15 to 20 minutes. Transfer the chicken to a cutting board and let it rest for 10 minutes.

Meanwhile, make the corn salad: Cut the kernels from the corncobs into a medium bowl. Add the shallot, oil, lime juice, basil, salt, and pepper and toss.

Cut the chicken into serving pieces and serve with the corn and basil salad.

Grilled Filet Mignon
with Summer Herb Sauce serves 4

I first made this recipe on a warm July evening for my father and me. We had spent the day working outside, and we were a little tired and very hungry. The filet mignon makes this otherwise simple main course feel sophisticated, while the rustic herb sauce stands up to the steak.

For the steak

2 fresh rosemary sprigs

1 tablespoon grainy mustard

2 garlic cloves, minced

1 tablespoon extra-virgin olive oil

¾ teaspoon kosher salt

¾ teaspoon black pepper

4 (6- to 8-ounce) filets mignons

For the sauce

1 small garlic clove

Kosher salt

2 cups mixed fresh herbs (dill, flat-leaf parsley, basil, thyme)

3 tablespoons extra-virgin olive oil

1 tablespoon apple cider vinegar

Black pepper

Marinate the steak: Remove the rosemary leaves from the stems and finely chop, discarding the stems. Stir together the rosemary with the mustard, garlic, oil, salt, and pepper. Rub the marinade all over the steaks.

Preheat the grill.

Meanwhile, make the sauce: Mince and mash the garlic to a paste with a pinch of salt, then transfer to a small bowl. Finely chop the herbs. Whisk the herbs, oil, vinegar, and ¼ teaspoon each salt and pepper with the garlic in the bowl. Season with additional salt and pepper to taste.

When the grill is hot, grill the steaks, turning occasionally to make crosshatched grill marks. Cook, covered, 8 to 10 minutes for medium-rare and 10 to 12 minutes for medium. Let the steaks rest for 10 minutes before serving.

Serve with the herb sauce on the side.

Beet, Blue Cheese, and Almond Salad serves 6

When I was a kid, we never ate beets, even though my grandfather always grew them, because my mother hated them. Now they're one of my favorite vegetables. Beets and blue cheese are a tried-and-true pairing for good reason. Here the beets are both cooked and grated raw, to add another dimension of flavor and texture to the salad.

7 large beets (2½ pounds)

1 small garlic clove

Kosher salt

3 tablespoons extra-virgin olive oil

2 tablespoons lemon juice

¾ teaspoon black pepper

8 ounces creamy blue cheese

2 ounces Marcona almonds

1 tablespoon chopped fresh flat-leaf parsley

Trim and peel the beets. Cut 6 of the beets into bite-sized pieces and place them in a steamer rack over a pot of boiling water. Cover the pot and steam the beets until they are tender, 25 to 30 minutes.

Coarsely grate the remaining beet into a bowl. Mash the garlic to a paste with a pinch of salt. Add the oil, lemon juice, garlic, 1 teaspoon salt, and the pepper to the grated beet. When the beets are cooked, toss them with the dressing and let them cool to room temperature.

Crumble the cheese over the beet salad and sprinkle with the almonds and parsley before serving.

Pennsylvania Dutch–Style Green Beans   serves 6

My grandmother's original recipe called for canned green beans. (She always had jars lining
the pantry that she canned herself.) My revisionist take made with fresh green beans is star-
tlingly delicious. The dressing, which uses milk, might seem a little odd to a modern cook's
sensibilities. It's a light version of a béchamel made sweet-and-sour with vinegar and brown
sugar.

1 pound green beans, trimmed and halved

4 slices bacon

1 medium onion, sliced

1 cup whole milk

2 tablespoons light or dark brown sugar

1 tablespoon cornstarch

½ teaspoon dry mustard

¾ teaspoon kosher salt

1 tablespoon apple cider vinegar or white distilled vinegar

1 hard-boiled egg (see page 41), chopped

Cook the beans in a large pot of boiling salted water until tender, about 6 minutes. Drain and transfer the beans to a bowl of ice water to stop the cooking, and drain again.

Cook the bacon in a large heavy skillet, turning, until it is crispy, 6 to 8 minutes. Transfer the bacon to a paper towel to drain. Reserve the fat in the pan.

Cook the onion in the bacon fat over medium heat until it is golden, 6 to 8 minutes.

Whisk together the milk, brown sugar, cornstarch, mustard, and salt, then whisk the milk mixture into the skillet with the onion and cook, stirring, until it comes to a boil. Boil the sauce until it is thickened, about 2 minutes. Whisk in the vinegar.

Place the beans in a serving dish and pour the sauce over the beans. Crumble the bacon. Sprinkle the bacon and egg over the top and serve.

String Beans with Herb Butter   serves 6 to 8

Sometime around the Fourth of July, I found myself standing knee-deep in weeds in the garden. Then things took a turn for the better. As I stood and stared, I noticed a single purple bean that had spiraled its way up and around a cluster of weeds: a pole bean. It was doing its best to choke out the weeds as it grew. I picked the beans from the stalk, and by the time I finished, I had about 2 pounds and I had forgotten all about the weeds. Instead of fretting, I made this dish. Quickly blanching the beans helps them retain their crunch and color, and the olive oil in the herb butter ensures the dressing will remain silky soft. This is a great dish to make ahead and serve at room temperature.

2 pounds mixed young string beans (haricots verts, pole beans, bush beans), trimmed

1 small shallot, finely chopped

3 tablespoons unsalted butter

1 tablespoon extra-virgin olive oil

1 cup chopped fresh herbs (basil, oregano, cilantro, dill, thyme)

1 teaspoon kosher salt

½ teaspoon black pepper

Blanch the beans in a large pot of boiling salted water until they are just tender, 4 to 8 minutes, depending on their size. Drain the beans, transfer them to a bowl of ice water to stop the cooking, and drain again.

Cook the shallot in the butter and oil in a small heavy skillet over low heat until the shallot is translucent, about 2 minutes. Let cool to room temperature, then toss the shallot and butter with the beans, herbs, salt, and pepper and serve.

Shredded Swiss Chard Salad   serves 4

This is one of my favorite salads, good with eggs for breakfast, pizza for lunch, or a summer barbecue for dinner. It's unusual to serve chard raw, but the leaves have a wonderful freshness, and they're easy to eat when sliced into very thin strands. The shredded mozzarella sprinkled over the salad reinforces the freshness of the greens. (Wrap the chard stems in plastic wrap and save them for Roasted Butternut and Chard Stem Hash, page 170.)

1 large bunch Swiss chard
   (12 ounces)

½ garlic clove

Kosher salt

2 tablespoons extra-virgin olive oil

1 tablespoon apple cider vinegar

1 tablespoon finely chopped shallot

1 fresh hot chile, very thinly sliced

Black pepper

5 ounces fresh mozzarella, coarsely grated (1½ cups)

Wash and dry the chard leaves. Remove the stems (see headnote), then stack the leaves in a pile, roll them up tightly, like a cigar, and thinly slice crosswise into very fine strands.

Mash the garlic to a paste with a pinch of salt. Whisk it with the oil, vinegar, shallot, chile, ½ teaspoon salt, and ¼ teaspoon pepper in a large bowl. Toss the chard in the vinaigrette. Sprinkle with the mozzarella, season the salad with salt and pepper to taste, and serve.

Easy Sautéed Chard   serves 4

When I need to get dinner ready fast, I cook greens using this technique: just mix 'em in a skillet with a little garlic and some bacon.

2 large bunches Swiss chard
   (1½ pounds)

2 slices thick-cut bacon, chopped

1 tablespoon extra-virgin olive oil

3 garlic cloves, thinly sliced

Kosher salt and black pepper

2 small scallions, thinly sliced

Separate the Swiss chard leaves from the stems. Cut the stems into 1-inch pieces.

Cook the bacon with the oil in a large heavy skillet over medium heat, stirring occasionally, until the bacon just starts to brown. Add the garlic, chard stems, ¾ teaspoon salt, and ½ teaspoon pepper and sauté, stirring occasionally, until the garlic is browned. Add the chard leaves by handfuls, turning over with tongs so they wilt evenly. Once the leaves are wilted, let them cook until the water they produce evaporates completely. Toss in the scallions, season with salt and pepper to taste, and serve.

Lemon-Garlic Swiss Chard serves 4

It's most common to cook chard stems and leaves separately (see Easy Sautéed Chard, page 126), but it doesn't always have to be that way—there's more than one way to cook a chard! You can steam the whole leaves, including their stalks, to make a simple veggie even simpler. Adding the garlic and lemon at the last minute gives this dish a superfresh finish.

1 garlic clove

Kosher salt

½ teaspoon finely grated lemon zest

1 tablespoon lemon juice

Black pepper

¼ cup water

1 large bunch Swiss chard (12 ounces)

2 tablespoons extra-virgin olive oil

Mash the garlic to a paste with ¼ teaspoon salt. Whisk the garlic together with the lemon zest, juice, and ¼ teaspoon each salt and pepper.

Bring the water to a boil in a large heavy pot over medium heat. Fold the bunch of chard in half and stuff it into the pot, then cover the pot. Let the chard steam until it is tender, 8 to 12 minutes. Uncover the pot and boil, letting the liquid evaporate completely. Transfer the chard to a cutting board and coarsely chop. Wipe out the pot.

Add the oil to the pot and heat over medium heat until it shimmers. Stir in the garlic-lemon mixture and cook it until the garlic is fragrant, about 1 minute.

Return the chard to the pot, tossing to combine. Season with salt and pepper to taste and serve.

Grilled Eggplant with Cilantro Pesto serves 6

Typically, pesto includes nuts of some sort, but this cilantro-coated vegetable dish doesn't need them, thanks to the rich texture of the eggplant. The smokiness from the grill infuses the eggplants, adding a deep complexity that is a delightful counterpoint to the bright, herby sauce and the sweet crunch of the onion. Think of it as a modern yet rustic, chunky take on baba ghanoush. This dish is great to make ahead, and I often serve it at room temperature.

2 (1- to 1½-pound) eggplants

4 tablespoons extra-virgin olive oil

Kosher salt and black pepper

1 garlic clove

2 cups cilantro leaves and stems

1 sweet onion, finely chopped

2 tablespoons lime juice

Preheat the grill and oil the grill rack.

Cut the eggplants in half lengthwise. Drizzle each cut side with ½ tablespoon oil, then sprinkle with ¼ teaspoon each salt and pepper.

Grill the eggplant halves over direct heat, turning occasionally, until they are charred in places and soft, 12 to 15 minutes. Transfer the eggplants to a serving plate and cover them with foil.

With the motor running, drop the garlic into a food processor and finely chop. Add the cilantro and the remaining 2 tablespoons oil and pulse until finely chopped. Season the pesto with salt and pepper to taste.

When the eggplant is cool enough to touch, scoop the flesh from the skins in chunks, discarding the skins, and toss the eggplant with the cilantro pesto, onion, lime juice, and salt and pepper to taste. Serve warm or at room temperature.

Potato Nachos serves 6

Potatoes are easy and fun to grow. Find a variety that you like (I'm partial to red, waxy potatoes) and save a few in the fridge until they start to sprout from their eyes. When you're ready to plant them, cut them in pieces so that each piece contains an eye with a sprout. Place those potato chunks in the ground, cover them with soil, and soon you'll have leafy plants and lots of little spuds. I can never wait until they're big; I always end up digging them when they're still small. Here, they stand in for nacho chips and come to the table drenched in melted cheese and a fresh tomato salsa. It's a great side dish or a hearty game snack.

4 pounds medium waxy potatoes

Kosher salt

1½ quarts vegetable oil

8 ounces grated sharp yellow cheddar cheese (2 cups)

8 ounces grated mozzarella cheese (2 cups)

4 ounces crumbled queso fresco, ricotta salata, or feta cheese (1 cup)

6 ounces sour cream (⅔ cup)

2 large ripe tomatoes, cored

½ white onion, chopped

2 tablespoons fresh lime juice

½ teaspoon black pepper

½ cup fresh cilantro leaves

Place the potatoes in a large pot with 1 tablespoon salt and cover with 2 inches cold water. Bring to a boil and cook until tender, about 30 minutes. Drain and let cool to room temperature. Using the palm of your hand, gently press down on each potato to lightly crush and expose the flesh while keeping the shape intact.

Preheat the oven to 300°F.

Heat the oil in a large cast-iron skillet or Dutch oven to 400°F. Fry the potatoes in batches until some of the exposed flesh is browned, 6 to 8 minutes per batch. (Return the oil to 400°F between batches.) Transfer the potatoes to paper towels to drain before placing them on an oven-proof serving platter.

Scatter the cheeses over the potatoes. Dollop the sour cream over them and place the platter in the oven until the cheese melts, about 10 minutes.

Meanwhile, chop the tomatoes, then combine with the onion, lime juice, ¾ teaspoon salt, and the pepper. Season with more salt to taste. Scatter the tomato salsa over the nachos, top with the cilantro, and serve.

Grilled Zucchini
with Fresh Tomato Vinaigrette   serves 6

The zucchini is grilled in big pieces, then chopped before being topped with a fresh vinaigrette made from ripe, juicy tomatoes.

3 large zucchini

3 tablespoons extra-virgin
 olive oil

1½ teaspoons kosher salt

1¼ teaspoons black pepper

1 garlic clove

1 sweet onion, chopped

2 medium tomatoes, chopped

¼ cup finely chopped fresh
 flat-leaf parsley

1 tablespoon lime juice

Preheat the grill and oil the grill rack.

Cut the zucchini in half lengthwise. Rub the cut sides with 1 tablespoon oil total, then sprinkle them evenly with 1 teaspoon salt and ¾ teaspoon pepper.

Grill the zucchini over direct heat, covered, turning occasionally, until slightly charred and soft all the way through, 6 to 10 minutes. Cut into 2-inch chunks.

Mince and mash the garlic to a paste with the remaining ½ teaspoon salt, then stir the garlic paste together with the onion, tomatoes, parsley, the remaining 2 tablespoons oil, lime juice, and the remaining ½ teaspoon pepper.

Place the zucchini on a serving plate, then top with the tomato vinaigrette and serve.

Zucchini with Their Flowers   serves 4

If you've ever grown your own zucchini, you know how far a few plants will go. This recipe is an easy and pretty way to celebrate the zucchini in all its forms, from flower to fruit.

4 medium zucchini

2 tablespoons extra-virgin olive
 oil, plus more for drizzling

Kosher salt

1 garlic clove, minced

¼ cup chopped cilantro

4 squash flowers, torn into pieces

Black pepper

½ cup finely grated Parmigiano-
 Reggiano

Cut the zucchini into ¼-inch rounds. Heat the oil in a large heavy skillet over medium-high heat until it starts to shimmer. Add the zucchini and ¾ teaspoon salt. Sauté the zucchini, stirring once or twice, until it is browned but not quite soft, 6 to 8 minutes.

Add the garlic to the skillet and sauté until it is fragrant, about 30 seconds. Remove the skillet from the heat and add the cilantro and squash flowers, tossing to combine. Season with salt and pepper to taste, then transfer to a serving plate. Drizzle with oil, sprinkle the Parmesan over the zucchini, and serve.

Cocoa-Zucchini Cake
with "Whipped Cream" Frosting   serves 8 to 10

All the chocolate fans *ooh* and *aah* when this comes out after dinner. If you've never thought to put zucchini in a cake, you'll be shocked by how much moisture it adds. (The batter also makes terrific cupcakes.) Carrot cake can't come close to this summer dessert.

The frosting for this cake was a fixture in my grandmother's kitchen, and my mother still raves about it as one of the best things she'd had when she first met my father. It uses the old-fashioned technique of thickening milk with flour to make it feel richer and more like cream. The result is a thick, buttery frosting.

For the cake

2 cups all-purpose flour

¾ cup unsweetened cocoa powder (not Dutch-process), plus more for dusting

1½ teaspoons kosher salt

1¼ teaspoons baking soda

2 sticks unsalted butter, at room temperature

1½ cups sugar

2 large eggs

1 teaspoon vanilla

1 cup water

8 ounces grated zucchini (1 medium)

For the frosting

1 cup whole milk

2½ tablespoons all-purpose flour

2 sticks unsalted butter, at room temperature

1 cup sugar

¼ teaspoon kosher salt

1 teaspoon vanilla

Make the cake: Preheat the oven to 350°F, with a rack in the middle. Butter and flour a 9-inch cake pan.

Whisk together the flour, cocoa powder, salt, and baking soda in a medium bowl.

Beat together the butter and sugar with an electric mixer until pale and fluffy, about 4 minutes. Add the eggs, one at a time, beating well, then beat in the vanilla. Add half of the flour mixture, the water, and then the remaining flour mixture, and finally the zucchini, mixing after each addition until just combined.

Pour the batter into the cake pan and smooth the top, then bake until a wooden pick inserted in the center comes out clean, 1 to 1¼ hours. Cool the cake in the pan on a rack for 1 hour.

Run a knife around the pan and invert the cake over a plate, then invert onto a serving plate.

Make the frosting: Whisk the milk and flour together in a small saucepan. Bring to a boil, whisking, then remove from the heat and let cool to room temperature. Cover the surface of the milk with waxed paper to prevent a skin from forming.

Beat the butter, sugar, and salt together with an electric mixer until the mixture is pale and fluffy. Beat in the milk mixture and beat until the frosting looks like whipped cream, at least 4 minutes. Beat in the vanilla.

Spread the frosting thickly over the cocoa-zucchini cake, dust with additional cocoa powder, and serve.

Magic Peach Cobbler   serves 6 to 8

There comes a time, right around the very middle of the summer, when peaches are everywhere. I can never quite get enough of them. Those that I don't eat right off the trees or can in honey syrup, I use in this old family recipe, which calls for fresh peaches and a hands-off approach to baking. The simplicity of this cobbler technique (in which sliced peaches are placed over a batter that puffs up around the fruit as it bakes) makes the delectable result seem almost magical. I serve this with ice cream.

1 stick unsalted butter

1 cup all-purpose flour

1 cup sugar

1½ teaspoons baking powder

½ teaspoon kosher salt

¾ cup whole milk

3 medium peaches

Preheat the oven to 350°F, with a rack in the middle.

Place the butter in a 3-quart baking dish and place it in the oven for 5 minutes, or until melted. Remove the dish from the oven, tilting the dish to evenly coat the bottom with the butter.

Whisk together the flour, ¾ cup of the sugar, the baking powder, and salt. Whisk in the milk. Pour the batter evenly over the butter in the baking dish. Do not stir.

Cut the peaches into wedges and place them in the batter. Sprinkle the remaining ¼ cup sugar over the top of the peaches. Bake the cobbler until it is set and golden on top, 35 to 40 minutes. Cool slightly on a rack.

Serve the cobbler warm or at room temperature.

A Jarful of Sunshine, a Bottleful of Sin

OUR GRANDMOTHER was a full-time mother of seven, and like many women of her era, she was a consummate canner. Many years after she died, our grandfather's pantry was still well stocked with the fruits of her labor. I am not nearly as prolific a preserver as she was. By next spring, all my canned tomatoes, pickled cucumbers, and aged garlic—ingredients for a happy winter—will be used up.

Skills like hers, sadly, have not been preserved. This became clear when I tried to buy canning jars and lids at the local Walmart. I wandered the aisles of the megastore in search of jars. They were not in the kitchen section. They were not in the food aisles, either. Finally, I asked an employee. Twenty minutes and three storewide pages later, we found them in the arts and crafts section. In a strange way, that location is appropriate. Canning is a craft and it is an art, a lost one—one that should be revisited and relearned by every American cook.

My grandmother's canned fruits and vegetables lasted so long not just because she was so prolific but because of the sentimental value they gained after she was gone. The jars were rarely opened. They were too special.

Once, in the breaking heat of July, as I finished mowing the last steep bank of the lawn with my T-shirt sticking to my back, the screen door to the porch swung open, and my grandfather called me in for lunch. I remember vividly what he offered me for dessert: a bowl of peaches. He said, "Mary made these."

He always called her Mary when he spoke of her, not Grandma or Granny. He had picked these peaches when they had been sun-kissed to perfection, and she had preserved them in syrup made using my grandfather's honey. They tasted like the sun and the bees. They tasted like they'd been made by hands that had raised seven children. They tasted like summer and the sweetest parts of love and life and family.

I still don't know why he chose that day to share the homegrown peaches with me. I could tell, even then, that it was a special moment. I tried my best to make them last, but they were too good. He offered me seconds, which I took.

Now, twenty-odd years later, I still feel the same way each time perfect peaches and honey hit my tongue. That love of summer, family, hard work, giving, cherishing, and sharing has been preserved in me.

The lesson I've learned: place the best of summer's fruits and vegetables in jars and share them with the people you love. In each jar, there is a special ingredient that everyone will taste, but no one will be able to identify. That extra something in there is the effort and love you put into the craft.

CANNING IS NOT THE ONLY WAY to save the fruits of the harvest. Tucked in the southernmost corner of the barn, in what used to be a granary, is an old hand-crank cider press. It's probably worth something to the right buyer. A quick Internet search found similar presses (circa 1880s) priced between $1,200 and $3,200. But like everything else here, including the farm itself, its only value is what it's worth to us. It's not for sale: we still use it every year. We have made cider from the apples of the ancient trees for as long as I've been alive. This year we finished apple-cider day with a measly twenty-five gallons. Many years we have upwards of fifty gallons, and the problem with fifty gallons of cider is you can't drink it fast enough, and it quickly starts to ferment.

We used to consider the cider's fermenting a bad thing. My grandparents, who scowled upon the wine at my father's dinner table, considered drinking a sign of weakness and sin. To them, the rotting apple juice lost its sweetness and tickled their tongues in a bad way with its effervescence. I imagine they thought the very liquid to be possessed with ungodliness as well. As such, it wasn't until very recently that it occurred to me to let the cider ferment, even to help it along. I'm sure there was some grave-rolling the moment that thought came to me.

Untreated apples, like ours, have what is called a bloom, a film that covers the skin of the fruit. So do grapes. Most people, thinking the bloom is dirt, try to wash it off. But it's not dirt, it's yeast, and if left alone, it will ferment the juice. A few years ago, I bought a five-gallon plastic bucket with a lid and filled it with five gallons of cider, fresh off the press. I covered it and placed it in the cellar of the farmhouse. In a month, it weighed in at about six percent alcohol, was crystal-clear, and as dry as the finest Champagne. It was also completely preserved and would last in bottles for years. But it didn't last that long, because we drank it.

WHEN THE GARDEN GIVES YOU TOO MANY tomatoes or cucumbers or zucchini, it's time to save them, with all their ripe flavors, while you can.

The equipment:

- A jar grabber to pick up the hot jars (looks like a large pair of tongs)
- A lid lifter (a stick with a magnet attached to one end so you can lift the lids out of the boiling water)
- A jar funnel (not really necessary, but it comes with canning kits)
- A canner (a large pot used to sanitize and seal the jars)
- Canning jars (½-pint, pint, or quart jars; Ball and Kerr make good-quality Mason jars)
- Lids (thin metal canning lids with a rubber ring that seals the lids onto the jars; these can be used only once)
- Rings (metal screw bands that secure the lids to the jars)

Another word for canning is processing, but don't let that scare you off. Canning is not that much of a process. It's really just a few simple steps. I like to keep the batches I make on the small side, a few pints or quarts, say, instead of tons and tons of jars, so that canning day doesn't ever feel overwhelming.

Whatever you're making, you'll want to start with the freshest produce, which, of course, is the whole point. If you find some blemishes or bruises, remove them.

If you want to try your hand at potted meats or low-acid foods, you'll need to invest in a pressure canner, but for now, let's stick to the basics.

When you're ready to fill your canning jars, wash the jars, lids, and rings with soap and hot water, then rinse them well. Place the jars and lids in the canner (or a large pot) and cover them with water. Bring the water to a boil. Remove the jars and lids with a jar grabber and a lid lifter and place them on a work surface lined with a clean kitchen towel.

Fill the jars as per the recipe, making sure to leave the recommended headspace.

Wipe off the rims of the filled jars with a clean, damp kitchen towel, then top with the lids and firmly screw on the rings.

Place the sealed jars back in the canner and cover them with water. Bring to a boil, covered.

Boil the jars for the time indicated in the recipe.

Lift the jars with the jar grabber and transfer them to a work surface to cool. The jars will seal (if you're in the kitchen, you'll hear the lids ping as they seal; it's a rewarding sound).

Press the center of each lid to make sure that it has sealed. Place any jars that have not sealed in the fridge and use them first. Store the sealed jars in a cool, dry, dark place.

The jars and rings may be used more than once, but you must use a new lid each time. Canning supplies are available at many hardware and big-box stores and by mail order from Ball (fresh-preserving.com). The *Ball Blue Book Guide to Preserving* is a helpful home-canning guide, and Ball even has a help line (800-240-3340).

Pickled Beets makes 6 pints

The first time I ever pickled beets, I had just graduated from high school and was helping my grandfather with his vegetable garden one summer weekend. He asked me if I liked beets, and I told him I wasn't sure, because we never ate them at home. He loaded four huge paper bags with them and then gave me and the veggies a ride to my parents' house. When we walked into the kitchen, my mother asked why we had brought them. My grandfather told her that no boy should grow up without beets. She rolled her eyes and told him that she hated them. My grandfather found that hilarious, and he spent the next few minutes laughing — before demanding that we cook all the beets that day. Much to Mom's chagrin, we started trimming the greens and breaking out the canning jars. That fall I left for college with jars and jars of pickled beets that would help feed me all semester. As she dropped me off at the dorm, Mom said she'd miss me, but not the beets.

6 pounds beets

6 fresh dill sprigs

3 shallots, sliced

2 tablespoons pickling spices

1½ cups distilled white vinegar

1½ cups water

1 cup sugar

2 tablespoons plus 1 teaspoon kosher salt

Preheat the oven to 400°F.

Wrap the beets in three separate packages of aluminum foil and roast until they are easily pierced with a knife, 1 to 1¼ hours. Let the beets cool to warm, then peel and slice them and divide them among 6 sterilized pint canning jars, along with the dill, shallots, and pickling spices.

Bring the vinegar, water, sugar, and salt to a boil. Pour the mixture over the beets, leaving ¼ inch of space at the top of the jars.

Cap the jars and process in boiling water for 20 minutes. Let the jars cool at room temperature until they seal. They will keep for at least a year in a cool, dry, dark place.

Refrigerator Radish Pickles makes about 1 pint

I always overdo it when I plant radishes. These pickles are an easy way to save them. Whenever I want a quick, crunchy appetizer or snack, I just pull them out of the fridge and put them in a bowl. That's it! Everyone always seems impressed, but they're dead easy. Not only do they keep practically forever in the fridge, they pick up more spice from the jalapeño as they sit. (Don't chuck your radish greens—use them for Pasta with Radishes and Blue Cheese, page 54.)

1 large bunch radishes (6 ounces), trimmed

1 tablespoon plus 1½ teaspoons kosher salt

1 cup distilled white vinegar

1 tablespoon sugar

1 jalapeño pepper

Cut the radishes in half, then toss with 1 tablespoon of the salt. Let them drain in a colander at room temperature for at least 1 hour.

Heat the vinegar with the sugar and the remaining 1½ teaspoons salt in a small saucepan over medium heat just until the sugar dissolves, about 1 minute (the vinegar does not need to come to a boil).

Rinse the radishes under cold running water, then pat them dry with a kitchen towel. Transfer them to a pint container. Pierce the pepper all over with a paring knife and add to the radishes. Pour the hot vinegar mixture over the radishes. Cool completely, then chill in the refrigerator for at least 2 days before serving.

These pickles keep, chilled, for at least 6 months.

Zucchini Relish   makes about 4 half pints

This is one of many sweet pickle recipes that my grandmother wrote down on an index card and filed. It's reminiscent of a chutney, and I often serve it as part of a cheese board. It's also great on burgers and hot dogs. My grandmother's original made four pints of relish, which is probably just the right amount if you're feeding seven children, as she was. I've cut the amounts in half and reduced the sugar slightly to let the flavor of the vegetables shine through.

Her recipe included an interesting technique. She salted her chopped vegetables and covered them with ice. The salting drew the water out of the veggies and concentrated their flavors, and the ice kept them cool in the unair-conditioned house, since her refrigerator was too small to hold them. As the ice melted, it also rinsed the excess salt from the veggies. If you have air-conditioning or available fridge space, just follow the recipe as written below. If not, try it my grandmother's way.

2 large zucchini (2 pounds total), chopped

1 large onion, chopped

1 red bell pepper, chopped

2 garlic cloves, smashed

2 tablespoons kosher salt

2 cups sugar

1½ cups apple cider vinegar or distilled white vinegar

½ cup water

1 tablespoon hot sauce (optional)

1 teaspoon turmeric

1 teaspoon mustard seeds

1 teaspoon celery seeds

¾ teaspoon black pepper

Toss the zucchini, onion, bell pepper, and garlic with the salt. Place the vegetables in a colander set over a bowl (or the sink) and let drain for 2 hours. Rinse the vegetables under cold running water, then pat dry.

Place the vegetables in a large heavy pot with the sugar, vinegar, water, hot sauce (if using), turmeric, mustard seeds, celery seeds, and pepper. Bring to a boil and boil the mixture until it is slightly thickened, 15 to 20 minutes.

Divide the relish among 4 sterilized half-pint canning jars while still hot, leaving ¼ inch of space at the tops. Cap the jars and process in boiling water for 10 minutes. Let the jars cool at room temperature until they seal. They will keep for at least a year in a cool, dry, dark place.

Dill Pickle Spears   makes 8 pints

Once you realize how easy it is to make your own pickles, you'll probably never go back to buying them. There is something very satisfying about cracking open a jar of homemade dill spears. Canning or pickling salt dissolves more easily in room-temperature water than kosher salt and is available at many grocery stores.

1¼ cups canning or pickling salt

2 gallons room-temperature water, plus 2 quarts for the brine

8 pounds Kirby cucumbers (about 5 inches long)

1½ quarts apple cider vinegar or distilled white vinegar

¼ cup sugar

2 tablespoons pickling spices

8 teaspoons mustard seeds

8 large fresh dill sprigs

Stir ¾ cup of the salt into the 2 gallons water until dissolved. Place the cucumbers in a large glass bowl, then pour the salt water over them. Let them stand at room temperature for 12 hours or overnight. Drain the cucumbers, discarding the liquid. Trim the ends from the cucumbers and discard, then slice the cucumbers lengthwise into spears.

Combine the vinegar, sugar, pickling spices, the remaining 2 quarts water, and the remaining ½ cup salt in a large heavy pot, then bring the pickling brine to a simmer.

Place 1 teaspoon mustard seeds and 1 dill sprig in each of 8 sterilized pint canning jars. Fill the canning jars with the cucumber spears, then pour the pickling brine over them, leaving ¼ inch of space at the tops. Cap the jars and process in boiling water for 10 minutes. Let the jars cool at room temperature until they seal. Let the pickles age for at least 1 week before opening. They will keep for at least a year in a cool, dry, dark place.

Tomato Sauce makes 2 quarts

There is many a cool fall or winter night when I don't feel like doing much in the kitchen. That's when these jars of summery, ripe tomato sauce come in especially handy. Just pop the top, heat the sauce in a skillet, and boil some pasta to toss with the sauce. After you start making your own sauce, you won't want to eat store-bought ever again.

6 pounds ripe tomatoes

3 tablespoons extra-virgin olive oil

2 tablespoons unsalted butter

2 large onions, chopped

6 garlic cloves, finely chopped

4 fresh oregano sprigs

1 fresh rosemary sprig

1 bay leaf

1 tablespoon sugar

1 mild fresh or dried red chile, chopped or crumbled

Kosher salt and black pepper

Score an X on the bottom of each tomato with a sharp knife. Plunge the tomatoes into a large pot of boiling water, in batches if necessary, until the scored Xs start to peel back, about 1 minute. Transfer the tomatoes with a slotted spoon to a large bowl of ice water and let them sit for a few minutes. Peel the tomatoes by slipping off the skins with your fingers and puree them in batches in a blender.

Heat the oil and butter in a large heavy pot over medium-high heat until hot. Stir in the onions and garlic and cook until they are browned, 10 to 12 minutes. Stir in the tomatoes, oregano, rosemary, bay leaf, sugar, chile, 2 teaspoons salt, and 1 teaspoon pepper. Bring the sauce to a boil and cook, stirring occasionally, until thickened, about 30 minutes. Remove the herb sprigs and bay leaf, then season the sauce with salt and pepper to taste.

Divide the sauce between 2 sterilized quart canning jars, leaving ¼ inch of space at the tops. Cap the jars and process in boiling water for 20 minutes. Let the jars cool at room temperature until they seal. They will keep for at least a year in a cool, dry, dark place.

Canned Tomatoes makes 4 quarts

Canning tomatoes is one of my favorite summer activities. We all work together in the breeze-filled kitchen of the farmhouse, peeling tomatoes and packing them into jars with a little salt and a fresh basil leaf. Then, inevitably, as the jars boil and seal away, someone makes cocktails and plays some music. It takes only a small part of an afternoon, but the dividends pay off all year, and each time I open one of those jars, I remember the day we canned them and how much fun it was.

12 pounds ripe tomatoes

4 fresh basil leaves

4 teaspoons kosher salt

Score an X on the bottom of each tomato with a sharp knife. Plunge the tomatoes into a large pot of boiling water, in batches, until the scored Xs start to peel back, about 1 minute. Transfer the tomatoes with a slotted spoon to a large bowl of ice water and let them sit for a few minutes.

Peel 1 tomato and puree it in a blender. Peel the remaining tomatoes by slipping off the skins with your fingers. Divide the tomatoes among 4 sterilized quart canning jars, along with 1 basil leaf and 1 teaspoon salt per jar, leaving ¼ inch of space at the tops. Top off the jars with pureed tomato, if necessary. Cap the jars and process in boiling water for 40 minutes. Let the jars cool at room temperature until they seal. They will keep for at least a year in a cool, dry, dark place.

Homemade Ketchup   makes 4 half pints

I slather ketchup on my eggs for breakfast. I smear it on every burger and dog. I dip fries and Cheese Grits Nuggets (page 6) in it. When I found a recipe for ketchup in one of my all-time favorite magazines, *Kitchen Gardener*, I made it immediately. I've been making my own adapted version ever since. Unfortunately, *Kitchen Gardener* ceased publication in the early 2000s. I have saved all my copies and still refer to them. If you can ever score an issue or two, do so.

1 teaspoon coriander seeds

1 teaspoon cumin seeds

1 teaspoon mustard seeds

1 bay leaf, broken into pieces

2 tablespoons extra-virgin olive oil

1 large onion, chopped

5 pounds ripe sauce tomatoes (Roma, San Marzano, Heinz 1350 VF)

1 tablespoon chopped fresh ginger

1 head roasted garlic, peeled (see page 78)

1 cup red wine vinegar or apple cider vinegar

¼ cup capers with brine

¼ cup hot sauce

2 tablespoons soy sauce

2 tablespoons Worcestershire sauce

⅓ cup dark brown sugar

2 teaspoons kosher salt

1 teaspoon paprika

½ teaspoon ground cinnamon

½ teaspoon ground allspice

½ teaspoon black pepper

Toast the coriander, cumin, and mustard seeds in a dry skillet over medium heat until they are several shades darker and very fragrant, about 2 minutes. Finely grind the seeds with the bay leaf in a spice grinder.

Heat the oil in a large heavy pot over medium-high heat until it shimmers. Add the onion and cook until well browned, about 10 minutes. Add the remaining ingredients, including the ground, toasted spices, and bring to a simmer. Simmer over low heat, stirring occasionally, until the vegetables have broken down, about 45 minutes.

Puree the ketchup, in batches if necessary, in a blender or food processor, then return it to the pot. Bring the ketchup back to a simmer and continue to cook until it reaches a paste-like consistency, 1½ to 2 hours more. Toward the end of cooking, stir the ketchup frequently to prevent scorching.

Divide the ketchup among 4 sterilized half-pint canning jars while still hot, leaving ¼ inch of space at the tops. Cap the jars and process in boiling water for 10 minutes. Let the jars cool at room temperature until they seal. They will keep for at least a year in a cool, dry, dark place.

Tomato Jam makes about 3 pints

Here's a fantastic way to spread your summer tomato crop out through the year. Once opened, the jam keeps for a couple of months in the fridge, and the Christmas-y spice here makes it just right when the weather turns cooler. I serve it with vanilla ice cream or simply spoon it inside prebaked tartlet shells and top it with whipped cream. This jam is also delicious spread on toast with butter.

2 pounds tomatoes (beefsteak, plum)

1 navel orange

1½ cups sugar

½ vanilla bean, split lengthwise

1 teaspoon apple cider vinegar

½ teaspoon ground cinnamon

¼ teaspoon freshly grated nutmeg

¼ teaspoon ground allspice

¼ teaspoon kosher salt

Score an X on the bottom of each tomato with a sharp knife. Plunge the tomatoes into a large pot of boiling water, in batches if necessary, until the scored Xs start to peel back, about 1 minute. Transfer the tomatoes with a slotted spoon to a large bowl of ice water and let them sit for a few minutes. Peel the tomatoes by slipping off the skins with your fingers, then trim the stem ends. Cut the tomatoes into large chunks. Quarter the orange, discarding any seeds, then slice as thinly as possible, including the rind.

Bring the tomatoes, orange slices, sugar, vanilla bean, vinegar, spices, and salt to a boil in a large heavy pot. Boil the jam, stirring occasionally, until thickened, 45 minutes to 1¼ hours.

To test the jam for doneness, drop a teaspoonful on a chilled plate and chill for 1 minute. Tilt the plate: the jam should remain in a mound and not run. If the jam runs, continue cooking it at a slow boil, testing every 5 minutes. Cool the jam completely.

Divide the jam among 3 sterilized pint canning jars, leaving ¼ inch of space at the tops. Cap the jars and process in boiling water for 15 minutes. Let the jars cool at room temperature until they seal. They will keep for at least a year in a cool, dry, dark place.

Strawberry-Cherry-Rhubarb Preserves

makes about 1 quart

I love this recipe for three reasons. First, it's flexible. Any combination of berries and rhubarb will do. If you have the strawberries, cherries, and rhubarb, then make it just the way my family has for generations. Great. But let's say that instead of cherries, you have blackberries. Use them instead!

The second reason is the technique that is used here. It might sound unusual to let the preserves sit at room temperature overnight, but this old-fashioned way to preserve the freshness of the fruit used to be quite common. After a quick boil (to kill any preexisting bacteria on the fruit), the sugar macerates the berries and preserves them. You're left with an intense freshness of flavor.

The last reason, and the best, is how these preserves taste. I serve them spooned over Cloud Biscuits (page 198), scones for breakfast, and ice cream for dessert.

1 quart mixed chopped strawberries, cherries, and rhubarb (see headnote)

2 cups sugar

2 teaspoons lemon juice

½ teaspoon kosher salt

Place the fruit in a dry heavy medium saucepan over medium heat. Bring to a boil, stirring, then remove from the heat. Stir in the sugar, lemon juice, and salt. Let the preserves sit at room temperature overnight or for up to 24 hours.

Place the preserves in jars and store in the refrigerator for up to a year.

Vinegar Chiles   makes about 2 cups

Every summer we get a huge crop of chiles—due mostly to my obsessive seed collecting throughout the year and my inability to plant fewer than forty plants in the spring. This is a quick and easy way to preserve chiles to make them last longer. Any combination of chiles works, but I love the floral notes that a habanero or two add to the mix.

I chop the pickled chiles and sprinkle them on everything from pizza and pasta to roast chicken. Don't ignore the vinegar that's left over. It's sharp and spicy and a great addition to vinaigrettes and sauces. A little goes a long way, though, so use it sparingly.

2 cups apple cider vinegar

¼ cup sugar

1 tablespoon kosher salt

8 ounces mixed hot chiles

1 small garlic clove, smashed

Heat the vinegar with the sugar and salt in a small saucepan over medium heat, stirring, until the sugar and salt are dissolved. Halve the chiles and place them, along with the garlic, in a sealable glass or plastic container, then pour the vinegar over the chiles. Keep the vinegar chiles, covered, in the refrigerator. They keep, chilled, for at least 6 months.

Hot Sauce   makes about 2¼ cups hot sauce and 1½ cups chile paste

I developed this recipe to use up all the chiles that I grow in the garden. After I made the hot sauce, I forgot about it in the back of the fridge. That turned out to be a happy accident, because this hot sauce keeps getting better with age. Feel free to use it right away, but if you tuck it away for a couple of months, even a year, the results will be stunning. Mixing several kinds of hot peppers together makes for an especially flavorful sauce. I use a combination of habanero, cayenne, serrano, Scotch bonnet, naga jolokia (much hotter than habanero), and whatever else I can find.

12 ounces hot red, orange, yellow, or green chiles, stemmed and halved

1 head roasted garlic, peeled (see page 78)

2¼ cups distilled white vinegar, plus more if needed

2 tablespoons light or dark brown sugar

2 tablespoons kosher salt

Place the chiles and roasted garlic in a food processor and pulse until finely chopped. Bring the vinegar, brown sugar, and salt to a simmer, stirring until the sugar is dissolved. Let the vinegar mixture cool completely. Place the chiles and garlic in a 1-quart glass jar, then add the vinegar mixture. Top off with additional vinegar, if necessary to cover the chiles. Cover the jar and refrigerate for at least 3 months and up to 1 year. Pour the hot sauce through a fine-mesh sieve. Use the liquid as hot sauce and the pulp as a chile paste. Keep both the hot sauce and the chile paste refrigerated.

Peaches in Honey Syrup makes 4 quarts

This dessert is so simple that most people would want to add some whipped cream or a cookie, but for me, there is nothing more delicious than eating peaches that have been preserved in honey syrup. The same thing happens every time I finish a bowl of these peaches: I take a fork and just keep eating them right from the jar.

12 pounds fresh peaches

2 cups water

1½ cups honey

8 cloves

1 teaspoon whole allspice

½ teaspoon kosher salt

Score an X on the bottom of each peach with a sharp knife. Plunge the peaches into a large pot of boiling water, in batches, until the scored Xs start to peel back, about 1 minute. Transfer the peaches with a slotted spoon to a large bowl of ice water and let them sit for a few minutes. Peel the peaches by slipping off the skins with your fingers, then halve them, discarding their pits.

Bring the water, honey, cloves, allspice, and salt to a boil.

Divide the peaches among 4 sterilized quart canning jars. Pour the honey syrup over the peaches, leaving ¼ inch of space at the tops. Cap the jars and process in boiling water for 40 minutes. Let the jars cool at room temperature until they seal. They will keep for at least a year in a cool, dry, dark place.

Quince "Honey" makes about 5 half pints

Quinces are practically inedible when raw, but once cooked, they become soft and sweet and have a flavor somewhere between an apple and a pear. Though there is no honey in this recipe, the color of the cooked preserves has a beautiful pale pink–golden hue that is reminiscent of it. The quince "honey" can be refrigerated or canned in half-pint jars and then stored for later use. It is my go-to breakfast jam for toast, and it also makes a great glaze for pork.

10 quinces

5 apples

4 cups water

5 cups sugar

¼ teaspoon kosher salt

Peel and core the quinces and apples, then cut the fruit into chunks. Combine the fruit with the water, sugar, and salt in a large heavy pot. Bring the mixture to a boil and cook, stirring occasionally, until thickened, about 1 hour. Transfer to a blender and puree in batches.

Divide the quince "honey" among 5 sterilized half-pint canning jars while still hot, leaving ¼ inch of space at the tops. Cap the jars and process in boiling water for 10 minutes. Let the jars cool at room temperature until they seal. They will keep for at least a year in a cool, dark place.

Cooked Pumpkin Puree   makes about 2 cups

As I was thumbing through a stack of my grandmother's handwritten recipe cards, I came upon a recipe called "Pumpkin Cake." The card itself had a 1960s cartoonish drawing of a cuckoo clock with toque-sporting bird, reminding me of my grandfather's collection of clocks, which would chime in unison every hour.

These days it's easy to buy canned pumpkin at the store, but my grandmother made her own pumpkin puree every fall and froze it (probably in 1-cup portions) to use in cakes and pies all winter. Now I devote a corner of my freezer to ziplock baggies, each containing 1-cup portions of cooked pumpkin puree. This recipe can be doubled, even tripled, and makes about 1 cup of puree for every pound of fresh pumpkin.

2 pounds pumpkin or winter squash

2 cups water

Halve the pumpkin and scoop out the seeds, then peel with a vegetable peeler or sharp knife. Cut the pumpkin into 2-inch chunks. Bring the water to a boil with the pumpkin in a heavy medium pot. Cook the pumpkin, covered, until it is very tender and starting to fall apart, about 20 minutes. Transfer the pumpkin to a food processor, discarding any remaining water in the pot. Puree the pumpkin until it is smooth, then return it to the pot. Bring the pumpkin back to a simmer over medium-low heat and cook, uncovered, stirring occasionally, until it is thick, 35 to 45 minutes.

Let the puree cool to warm. Use immediately or freeze portions in small ziplock bags. They keep for at least 6 months.

Hard Cider makes about 4½ gallons

Ever since my late twenties, I've been setting aside about five gallons of cider every fall to drink as hard cider the following summer. Making hard cider is one of the easiest things to do. Apples (so long as they have not been sprayed with fungicide) have what's called a bloom, a very thin, barely visible layer of wild yeast on their skins. That yeast is all that's needed to start the fermentation of the fresh apple cider. So if you're lucky enough to have organic, unsprayed apples and a press, you're in business. Just press out the apple juice, place it in a glass carboy (available at homebrew supply stores) fitted with an airlock, and leave it alone. In a few months, you'll have delicious hard apple cider.

This recipe uses Champagne yeast (again: homebrew supply) to jump-start the fermentation.

If you're new to brewing, you'll need some equipment to get started. All of it is available at homebrew supply stores (my favorite store is Brooklyn Homebrew, 718-369-0776, www. brooklyn-homebrew.com).

1 (5- to 6-gallon) glass carboy

Sanitizing solution

1 rubber stopper to fit carboy

1 airlock

1 (5-gallon) plastic bucket

Plastic tubing for siphoning

About 48 (12-ounce) bottles

48 crown bottle caps

1 crown capper

5 gallons raw (unpasteurized) apple cider at room temperature, plus 1 pint fresh cider for bottling

1 (12-gram) package Champagne yeast

Clean the carboy with sanitizing solution. Fill the carboy with the 5 gallons of cider and pitch the yeast over the top. Top the carboy with the stopper and place the airlock in the stopper. Top the airlock with water. Let the cider ferment at 65° to 75°F for at least 2 months. Clean the plastic bucket and plastic tubing with sanitizing solution, then siphon the cider from the carboy to the bucket, leaving the sediment on the bottom of the carboy.

Stir the 1 pint fresh cider into the fermented cider (this will add enough fermentable sugar to create carbonation in the bottles). Clean the bottles and caps with sanitizing solution, then fill and cap the bottles using the crown capper. Let stand at room temperature for at least 3 weeks before chilling and drinking. The bottled cider will keep for several years in a cool, dry, dark place.

Hard Cider

A Cool Change in the Breeze

STARTED MY HOT PEPPER PLANTS in March. By all accounts, it was too early in the year, but I couldn't help myself. I had saved seeds from my favorite peppers: there was one from a trip to Brazil; one from Tim Stark, a famous pepper farmer who sold his wares in New York City's Greenmarket; and one that the writer Barry Estabrook had smuggled back from Jamaica. Each pepper had a story. Every day I stood over the window box where I'd planted them, checking the plants' progress. They had grown to a full three inches by late April.

They were the first plants I placed in the ground when we planted the garden in May, and I gave them more space than I thought they would need. I watered them diligently and weeded constantly. Nothing happened. The pepper plants refused to grow. By June, when every other plant in the garden had skyrocketed, they were still only four inches tall. I started to get nervous.

I stopped by Tim's Greenmarket stand and asked his right-hand man, Wayne, what I should do. Wayne told me the weather had been too cool. These were tropical plants, after all, and they needed more sun than what was available in Pennsylvania in the early summer. Wayne counseled patience. So I waited.

And waited.

It wasn't until September that I noticed the pepper plants had grown to a height of three feet and were loaded with fiery fruits. They dangled like Christmas ornaments on a tree, their colors smoldering against the garden's green backdrop. I plucked a chocolate habanero from the plant and took a small bite. I burst into an instant sweat. My eyes felt as if they had crossed. My belly burned as if from whiskey. I took another bite from the pepper, then picked all that were ripe—about 3 pounds—and researched recipes for hot sauce.

• • •

THE WALNUT TREES had started to drop their nuts, thudding to the ground all around the farm with a whomping sound like a bass drum, in a rhythm like a syncopated requiem for summer. By the time they began, the orchestra was already rising to a crescendo, and no conductor had the power to stop it.

On cue, the days became shorter, the leaves started to turn the colors of sunsets, and there was an unfamiliar chill on the edge of the dark night air. The peppers in their hued extravagance cried out to be saved. I dried the seeds from my favorite peppers and placed them in waxed paper bags, ready to placate my impatience in the coming March.

It might seem that this time of year, after summer has stepped away and before the cold of late fall and winter has set in, is a sort of no-man's-land—the brunch of the seasons. But it is not. It should have its own name. Sumall, maybe, or falummer or fummer. None of those names, though, do these few weeks justice.

Whatever we call it, like brunch, this short season is a wonderful time to eat. Foods that are too heavy for the heat of the summer, like fried chicken, start to taste good again. One evening, I realized I was out of flour. The only substitute I could find in the pantry was cornmeal, so I coated the chicken with it, letting some of the spices from the liquid I had brined the chicken in tag along for the ride, tucked into the flaps of the meat and skin. This was a whole new (and better) fried chicken. We ate it by the bucketful, alongside a big steaming pot of long-braised collard greens and roasted butternut squash and Swiss chard.

The butternut squash was also an eye-opener. When I tasted it, it suddenly dawned on me the reason for its name. It tasted like butter! And nuts! And squash! I started telling everyone I met who had a garden to grow butternut. They stared at me as though I were claiming to have invented the question mark. But the fog had been lifted, and I was preaching the butternut gospel, waving a seed package high in the air. In comparison, industrially grown butternut tastes as if it has been put through a deflavorizer. The same is true of kale, a vegetable I had to choke down as a child. The kale we grow tastes green in the best way and is flavorful enough to eat raw when tossed with a vinaigrette and some toasted walnuts.

Our hearty in-between-season dinner was marked by another special event: it was cool enough to light a fire. The wood smoke added intrigue and comfort to every bite.

Coriander Seed–Cornmeal Fried Chicken serves 4

It took me years to get this recipe just right, but it is, at last, my ultimate fried chicken. The coriander seeds that stick to the meat after it is brined burst with intense flavor when you bite through the crisp cornmeal crust. Watch out, Colonel, this chicken just might collapse your empire. Serve this with Creamy Long-Cooked Collards (page 173) for a deeply satisfying meal.

Organic chickens are considerably smaller than nonorganic chickens. They also taste better. (The variation between the thigh sizes of the two is the reason for the wide cooking-time range in the recipe.)

4 cups water

2 bay leaves

2 teaspoons coriander seeds, crushed

1 teaspoon dried thyme

½ teaspoon dried red pepper flakes

1 garlic clove, smashed

2 tablespoons plus 1 teaspoon kosher salt

8 chicken thighs (about 2½ pounds total)

1½ cups fine cornmeal

1½ teaspoons paprika

¾ teaspoon black pepper

About 5 cups vegetable oil

Bring the water, bay leaves, coriander, thyme, red pepper flakes, garlic, and 2 tablespoons of the salt to a simmer in a heavy medium saucepan. Let the brine cool to room temperature. Pour the brine over the chicken in a bowl, then refrigerate for at least 3 hours or overnight.

Remove the chicken from the brine, letting as many coriander seeds stick to the chicken as possible. (I even tuck them under the skin and into the crevices of the exposed meat; the more, the better.)

Stir together the cornmeal, paprika, the remaining 1 teaspoon salt, and the pepper in a shallow bowl. Coat the chicken thoroughly with the cornmeal mixture, place it on a rack, and let it sit at room temperature while the oil heats.

Heat the oil in a 6-quart pot to 400°F. Add half of the chicken and fry, turning the pieces over occasionally, until they are golden brown and cooked through, 10 to 18 minutes, depending on the size of the thighs. Drain on paper towels and bring the oil back to 400°F. Fry the remaining chicken in the same way, drain, and serve.

Quick Coq au Vin   serves 4 to 6

This French countryside meal has become something of an American standard, too, thanks in large part to Julia Child. America has been producing world-class red wines for decades, and I love using a big, fruity California Zinfandel in this recipe. It brings a boldness to the dish that gives it a New World sensibility. Of course, it's deliberate that the recipe uses only 1½ cups wine, leaving the rest for the cook.

1 (3½-pound) chicken, cut into serving pieces

Kosher salt and black pepper

1 tablespoon extra-virgin olive oil or Master Fat (page 23)

1 medium onion, chopped

2 carrots, sliced

1 celery stalk, chopped

5 garlic cloves, smashed

1½ cups dry red wine, such as California Zinfandel

2 bay leaves

1 fresh thyme sprig

Pat the chicken dry and season it with 1½ teaspoons salt and ½ teaspoon pepper. Heat the oil in a large heavy skillet over medium-high heat until it shimmers. Sear the chicken, skin side down, until it is golden brown (do not turn it over), 3 to 6 minutes. Transfer the chicken to a plate.

Add the onion, carrots, celery, and garlic to the skillet and cook, scraping up any browned bits, until the vegetables are golden, about 6 minutes. Add the wine, bay leaves, and thyme and bring to a boil.

Return the chicken to the skillet, skin side up, and simmer, covered, until it is cooked through, 20 to 25 minutes. Uncover the skillet and simmer until the liquid is slightly reduced, 3 to 5 minutes. Discard the bay leaves. Season with salt and pepper to taste and serve in shallow bowls.

Herb-Roasted Lamb Shanks   serves 4

By fall we are desperately searching for ways to use up our dried herbs from last summer so we can restock with this summer's herbs, which I cut and dry by hanging them in the barn. This recipe uses a fair amount of mixed herbs, an intense, aromatic reminder of the summer's bounty coupled with the smoldering intrigue of smoked paprika. (American-made smoked paprika is available in many supermarkets, while Spanish smoked paprika — the best is Pimentón de la Vera — can be purchased at gourmet markets or online.) Instead of stock, water is used as a braising liquid. The resulting pan juices from the herbaceous rub are so flavorful that you don't need wine or stock.

¼ cup extra-virgin olive oil

¼ cup mixed dried herbs (rosemary, lavender, thyme, oregano)

1½ teaspoons ground cinnamon

1 teaspoon smoked paprika (see headnote)

½ teaspoon freshly grated nutmeg

Kosher salt and black pepper

4 (1-pound) lamb shanks

2 cups water

Stir together the oil, herbs, cinnamon, paprika, nutmeg, 2 teaspoons salt, and ¾ teaspoon pepper. Pat the lamb dry, then rub all over with the herb mixture.

Preheat the oven to 350°F.

Heat a dry large cast-iron skillet over medium-high heat, then brown the lamb shanks on one side, 5 to 8 minutes. Turn the shanks over and add the water to the skillet. Cover the skillet tightly, then place it in the oven for 2 hours. Uncover the skillet and roast until the meat is very tender and most of the liquid in the pan has evaporated, about 1 hour more. Season with salt and pepper to taste and serve the lamb with the pan juices.

Hot Pepper–Garlic Flank Steak
with Quick Cucumber and Chile Pickles serves 4

Chiles and garlic transform common flank steak, adding pungency and capsicum to each bite. The pickles are fantastic when they're on the same fork as the meaty, chile-rubbed steak, and they take just 15 minutes to throw together.

For the steak

2 hot chiles (habanero, jalapeño, or serrano)

4 garlic cloves, finely chopped

1 teaspoon chili powder

3 tablespoons extra-virgin olive oil

1 teaspoon kosher salt

¾ teaspoon black pepper

1 (2-pound) flank steak

For the pickles

1 medium cucumber

1 medium red onion

2 hot chiles (habanero, jalapeño, or serrano)

⅓ cup apple cider vinegar or distilled white vinegar

2 tablespoons sugar

1 teaspoon kosher salt

¾ teaspoon black pepper

Marinate the steak: Finely chop the hot chiles, including the seeds and ribs for extra heat. Stir together the chiles, garlic, chili powder, 2 tablespoons of the oil, the salt, and pepper. Rub the pepper mixture all over the steak and let marinate, chilled, for at least 1 hour.

Meanwhile, make the pickles: Peel the cucumber and cut it in half lengthwise. Remove the seeds, then thinly slice it crosswise. Thinly slice the onion and chiles. Combine the vegetables with the vinegar, sugar, salt, and pepper. Let the pickles stand at room temperature until ready to use.

Heat the remaining 1 tablespoon oil in a large heavy skillet over medium-high heat until the oil just begins to smoke. Sear the steak, turning over once, until well browned and cooked to the desired doneness, 8 to 10 minutes for medium-rare.

Remove the steak from the skillet and let stand for 10 minutes before slicing. Serve the steak with the quick pickles.

Butternut–Caramelized Onion Pizza serves 4 to 6

I got the idea for this pizza one early-fall evening as I stood in the kitchen staring at about a dozen butternut squash. I wanted to come up with a dish that used the squash in an unusual way, and just like that, this pizza was born. It has been a go-to fall Friday-night dinner ever since. Calling it a pizza doesn't really do this awesome flatbread justice. It's more like a party on pizza dough: the sweetness of the onions and the color of the squash make everyone smile. Slicing the butternut squash as thinly as possible helps it cook in a flash, and the quick-pickled chile adds a subtle heat that acts as a counterpoint to the rich cheese and sweet onions. Serve with Chile Vinegar–Parsley Salad (page 221) for a meal that is both satisfying and bright. If you've made the Vinegar Chiles (page 153), you can skip the directions for the quick-pickled chile and use one from your fridge.

4 medium onions, sliced

6 tablespoons extra-virgin olive oil

Kosher salt

1 fresh hot chile, finely chopped (see headnote)

2 tablespoons apple cider vinegar

1½ pounds Pizza Dough (page 113)

1 pound butternut squash, from the top half of the squash

1 teaspoon fresh thyme leaves

½ teaspoon black pepper

8 ounces shredded Monterey Jack cheese

Cook the onions with 2 tablespoons of the oil and ½ teaspoon salt in a large heavy skillet over medium heat, covered, for 15 minutes. Uncover the skillet and continue to cook, stirring more and more frequently as the onions caramelize, until they are golden brown, 25 to 30 minutes more.

Preheat the oven to 500°F, with a rack in the lowest position. If you have a pizza stone, place it on the rack.

Place the chile in a small bowl with the vinegar and a pinch of salt.

Spread 2 tablespoons of the oil on a large baking sheet and stretch the pizza dough to fit the pan, letting the dough rest between stretches. It will feel tight at first, but will relax as you continue to stretch it.

Spread the onions evenly over the dough.

Peel the squash and cut it crosswise as thinly as possible with an adjustable slicer or a very sharp knife, then toss it with the remaining 2 tablespoons oil, the thyme, ½ teaspoon salt, and the pepper. Place the squash over the onion layer, overlapping the slices slightly. Drain the chile, then sprinkle the chile over the squash. Sprinkle the cheese evenly over the pizza, then bake, rotating the pan halfway through, until the crust is browned and the cheese is melted and bubbling, 20 to 30 minutes. Serve.

Raisin-Caper Broccoli   serves 4

The best part of broccoli is its stems. The florets are fine, but it's the meaty stems that really do it for me, so when I grow broccoli, I look for the plants that have more stem and less head (I do the same when I buy broccoli from the farmers' market). This recipe uses a couple of very flavorful ingredients (raisins and capers) to add a sweet and briny contrast, while the bread crumbs add a nice crunch.

2 pounds broccoli

¼ cup extra-virgin olive oil

⅔ cup panko (Japanese bread crumbs)

⅓ cup raisins

2 tablespoons drained capers, chopped

1 garlic clove, finely chopped

Kosher salt and black pepper

Peel the broccoli stems and coarsely chop the stems and florets. Cook the broccoli in boiling salted water until just tender, 4 to 6 minutes. Drain the broccoli.

Heat the oil in a large heavy skillet until it shimmers. Add the panko, raisins, capers, garlic, ½ teaspoon salt, and ¼ teaspoon pepper and cook, stirring occasionally, until the panko and garlic are golden, 3 to 4 minutes.

Just before serving, toss the broccoli with the panko mixture and season with salt and pepper to taste.

Roasted Butternut and Chard Stem Hash   serves 4

I love using all the parts of a vegetable (like the broccoli stems in Raisin-Caper Broccoli, above, or squash flowers in Zucchini with Their Flowers, page 131). Shredded Swiss Chard Salad (page 126) uses only the leaves, so be sure to save those chard stems for this hash — they're incredibly flavorful, and their earthiness pairs well with the sweetness of the squash.

1 (2½-pound) butternut squash

2 tablespoons extra-virgin olive oil

Kosher salt and black pepper

2 bunches (about 1 pound) Swiss chard stems, chopped

1 garlic clove, minced

Preheat the oven to 425°F.

Peel and seed the squash and cut it into ½-inch pieces. Place the squash on a baking sheet, then drizzle with the oil and sprinkle with ¾ teaspoon salt and ½ teaspoon pepper. Toss the squash with your hands to distribute the oil and seasonings well. Roast, stirring the squash occasionally with a spatula, until it is beginning to brown, 25 to 30 minutes.

Stir the Swiss chard stems and the garlic in with the squash, then return to the oven and roast until the chard stems are tender, 15 minutes more. Season the hash with salt and pepper to taste and serve.

Thyme-Roasted Butternut Squash serves 4 to 6

When butternut squash are ripe (you can tell by the hollow sound they make when you tap them), they are unbelievably sweet and nutty, with a smooth, buttery flavor. This recipe keeps things simple by roasting the squash with oil, thyme, salt, and pepper, then generously sprinkling it with cheese. It may seem like a lot of cheese at first, but once everything gets mixed together, the salty cheese and the fresh thyme do a great job of balancing the inherent sweetness of the squash.

1 (3-pound) butternut squash

¼ cup extra-virgin olive oil

2 teaspoons chopped fresh thyme

Kosher salt and black pepper

⅔ cup finely grated Parmigiano-Reggiano

Preheat the oven to 425°F, with racks in the upper and lower thirds.

Peel and seed the squash and cut it into ½-inch pieces. Toss the squash with the oil, thyme, ¾ teaspoon salt, and ½ teaspoon pepper and divide between two large baking sheets.

Roast the squash, stirring occasionally, until it is tender and browned, 25 to 30 minutes. Transfer the squash to a serving bowl and sprinkle generously with the Parmesan. Season with salt and pepper to taste and serve.

Kale and Toasted Walnut Salad serves 4

It's hard to believe this salad is so delicious, since it seems so simple, but the secret is fresh (as in garden-fresh) kale. The salad lets kale be just what it is: full-bodied and hearty. Serving it raw is not that common in this country, but after one bite, I'm sure you'll agree: this is kale like you've never had it before.

8 ounces kale (preferably lacinato, aka dinosaur kale)

1 tablespoon lemon juice

2 tablespoons extra-virgin olive oil

Kosher salt and black pepper

4 ounces black or English walnuts, toasted

½ cup finely grated Parmigiano-Reggiano

Remove and discard the ribs from the kale and tear the leaves into 2-inch pieces. Put the kale in a serving bowl and toss with the lemon juice, oil, ½ teaspoon salt, and ¼ teaspoon pepper. Sprinkle the salad with the walnuts and Parmesan, season to taste with salt and pepper, and serve.

Creamy Long-Cooked Collards serves 6

Collard greens are hearty and full of flavor. This recipe treats them in a classic Southern way by braising them with a ham hock until they're supersoft and finishing the broth with some cream. The result is a satisfying side dish to any meat. The recipe is absolutely worth the time it takes to braise the greens; they cook until their texture becomes so silky that they melt in your mouth. Ask your butcher to cut the ham hock in half so the bone's exposed; you'll get even more meaty flavor out of it. (For a totally different and extremely fast way to cook collards, check out Pasta with Shredded Collard Greens, page 212.)

4 ounces sliced bacon

2 medium onions, sliced

2 garlic cloves, thinly sliced

Kosher salt and black pepper

1 cup water

¼ cup apple cider vinegar

2 tablespoons light or dark brown sugar

2½ pounds collard greens, thick stems discarded and leaves coarsely chopped

1 ham hock, halved

1 cup heavy cream

Cook the bacon in a heavy medium pot over medium heat until it is brown and crisp, turning occasionally, about 8 minutes. Transfer the bacon to a paper towel to drain, reserving the fat in the pot.

Cook the onions and garlic in the bacon fat with 1 teaspoon salt and ½ teaspoon pepper, stirring occasionally, until the onions are browned, 8 to 10 minutes. Stir in the water, vinegar, and brown sugar, scraping up any browned bits. Add the collards and ham hock. Cover the pot and cook, stirring occasionally, until the collards are silky and very tender, about 40 minutes. Stir in the cream, bring to a boil, and boil until the liquid is almost completely evaporated, about 15 minutes. Remove the ham hock from the pot and place on a cutting board. Remove any meat from the ham hock, discarding the bones. Chop the meat, then add the ham to the collards. Season the collards with salt and pepper to taste.

Crumble the bacon over the collards and serve.

Mustardy Mustard Greens serves 4

I'm always trying to come up with ways of cooking greens that make everyone want to dive right in (especially the younger members of the family, who might not yet know how wonderful leafy greens can be). Once they've tried these, there's no stopping the feeding frenzy. Think of the dish as mustard three ways: mustard seeds, mustard greens, and Dijon. Serve this with Coriander Seed–Cornmeal Fried Chicken (page 164) and white rice or some baked potatoes, and call it a night.

1½ pounds mustard greens

3 tablespoons extra-virgin olive oil

1 large onion, chopped

3 large garlic cloves, minced

Kosher salt and black pepper

1 teaspoon mustard seeds

1½ tablespoons Dijon mustard

1½ tablespoons apple cider
   vinegar

1½ teaspoons sugar

¼ cup sliced almonds, toasted

Remove and discard the ribs from the mustard greens and tear the leaves into large pieces. Boil the greens in a pot of well-salted boiling water until they are crisp-tender and have lost their bitter taste, 3 to 5 minutes. Drain the greens, and when they are cool enough to handle, press on them to extract excess liquid.

Heat the oil in a large heavy skillet over medium heat until it shimmers. Add the onion, garlic, ¾ teaspoon salt, and ½ teaspoon pepper and cook until the onion is golden, about 5 minutes. Add the mustard seeds and continue to cook for 1 minute more. Remove the skillet from the heat and add the Dijon, vinegar, and sugar, stirring to combine. Stir in the mustard greens. Season with salt and pepper to taste. Serve the mustard greens sprinkled with the almonds.

Silky Eggplant Puree   serves 4 as a side dish or hors d'oeuvre

I'm always happy to cook with eggplant from the garden. This puree—like a creamy, country version of baba ghanoush—is good alongside Herb-Roasted Lamb Shanks (page 166), or as a dip for veggies and pita bread. It keeps well in the fridge, so you can have a bunch on hand for snacking or last-minute hors d'oeuvres.

2 (1- to 1½-pound) eggplants

2 tablespoons extra-virgin olive oil

Kosher salt

1 head roasted garlic (see page 78)

1 teaspoon finely grated lemon zest

1 tablespoon lemon juice

1 tablespoon finely chopped fresh flat-leaf parsley

Black pepper

Preheat the oven to 450°F. Oil a large baking sheet.

Trim the eggplants and halve them lengthwise. Rub them all over with the oil, then sprinkle the cut sides with 1 teaspoon salt total. Place the eggplants, cut side down, on the baking sheet and roast until very tender, 40 to 45 minutes. Remove from the oven and let cool to warm. (If you don't have the roasted garlic on hand, roast it now.)

Scrape the eggplant flesh from the skins, discarding the skins. Peel the roasted garlic cloves. Puree the eggplant in a blender with the roasted garlic cloves, lemon zest, and juice. Transfer to a serving dish, fold in the parsley, and season with salt and pepper to taste. Serve warm or at room temperature.

Pumpkin Cake
with Bourbon-Caramel Sauce serves 10 to 12

This recipe has been adapted from the handwritten recipe card of my grandmother. I've made a few changes to make it a little less old-fashioned. The unusual thing about this cake is that it does not rely on spices to cover the flavor of the squash. When you take a bite, you taste pure, unadulterated pumpkin.

The walnuts my grandmother used were probably black walnuts collected from the trees at the farm, but since they're difficult to find (and shell), I often use regular English walnuts, which I toast for extra flavor. I've added a maple–cream cheese frosting and a bourbon-caramel sauce — exactly what this old-time recipe needed.

For the cake

1 stick unsalted butter, at room temperature

1 cup sugar

1 cup light brown sugar

2 large eggs

1 cup Cooked Pumpkin Puree (page 156)

3 cups sifted cake flour (sifted before measuring)

1 tablespoon baking powder

½ teaspoon kosher salt

½ cup whole milk

1 cup walnut pieces, toasted

1 tablespoon maple syrup

For the sauce

1 cup sugar

2 tablespoons water

⅓ cup bourbon

1 cup heavy cream

Large pinch kosher salt

2 tablespoons unsalted butter

Make the cake: Preheat the oven to 350°F, with a rack in the middle. Butter and flour a 13-by-9-inch baking pan.

In a large bowl, beat together the butter, sugar, and brown sugar with an electric mixer until it comes together. Beat in the eggs, one at a time, until the mixture is pale and fluffy. Beat in the pumpkin puree (the mixture will look curdled). In a medium bowl, whisk together the flour, baking powder, and salt. Add half of the flour mixture to the pumpkin mixture, mixing until it is just combined. Mix in the milk, then the remaining flour mixture. Fold in the walnuts and maple syrup.

Pour the batter into the pan and bake until a tester or a toothpick inserted in the center comes out clean, 45 to 55 minutes. Cool the cake completely in the pan on a rack.

Make the sauce: Before you start, make sure anything flammable is moved away from the area near your stove.

Bring the sugar and water to a boil in a heavy medium skillet over medium heat. Cook, swirling the skillet for even browning, until the caramel is a golden amber color, 8 to 10 minutes. Add the bourbon and carefully ignite by tilting the skillet toward the flame (or, if you have an electric stovetop, use a kitchen match). Let the alcohol burn off completely, then immediately add the cream and salt. Simmer the sauce until the caramel is dissolved and the sauce is thickened, about 5 minutes. Remove the skillet from the heat and whisk in the butter.

For the frosting

8 ounces cream cheese, at room temperature

½ stick unsalted butter, at room temperature

¼ cup maple syrup

1 tablespoon light or dark brown sugar

Make the frosting: Beat together the cream cheese, butter, maple syrup, and brown sugar with an electric mixer until it is fluffy, about 2 minutes. Spread the frosting over the cake.

Just before serving, make a pool of sauce on the plate, then top with the cake and serve.

Loving, Learning, and a Ton of Hard Work

W HEN I WAS SIXTEEN, I took a month off from my farm chores to travel to Germany as part of an exchange program. There, I was able to gain a basic understanding of the language and leave my sweat-filled summer duties stateside. But part of me missed my grandfather. I remember feeling worried that I'd lose the old man, that he might prematurely kick the bucket while I selfishly drank beer and ate wurst. On the flight home from Europe, I stared out the window of the airplane and teared up a bit. In German, there is a word for that kind of sadness: *traurigkeit*. I was sad, and unnecessarily so. He was fine.

The morning after coming home, I went directly to visit him and, by noon, was almost finished mowing his four-acre lawn. By then it was hot, and I was hungry. Like most men of his day, my grandfather never cooked, so I was surprised when he called me off the lawn with a brisk wave of his arm. He'd made me a sandwich; the only time he ever prepared me anything. And I believed then, as I do now, that he made me lunch that day as a way to show that he'd missed me, too. It's a sandwich I'll never forget, and not just because he made it. It was also delicious.

Salted butter, summer-kitchen soft, was thickly spread over white bread, then layered generously with Lebanon bologna—a sweetened, cured meat popular in Pennsylvania Dutch country—and topped with cold, crisp iceberg lettuce. I can still taste the salty-sweet play between the butter and the bologna. I can still hear the cooling crunch of the lettuce and remember the squish of the white bread. And I can still feel the warmth of the sun and my grandfather's smile as he watched me devour the sandwich.

Almost exactly sixteen years after that, I stared out the window of another airplane. I was returning from Brazil with a basic grasp of the language and a slight case of dysentery. This time I was flying home for my grandfather's funeral, but all I could think about was that sandwich.

Unlike German, Portuguese is a beautiful language. There are words with meanings so complex that they can be translated only by using full sentences. One of them, *saudade*, expresses a longing for a person—not in a sad way, but fondly. One definition describes it as "the recollection of feelings, experiences, places, or events that once brought excitement, pleasure, well-being, which triggers the senses and makes one live again." Now *that* is a word.

I have *saudade* for my grandfather. He lived a full and happy life, and the many lessons, memories, and skills that I learned from him have helped me live a full, happy life, too.

I still make bologna sandwiches for the people I love. The last time was a freezing fall day, for Leif, my father, and my cousin Gavin. Once again, the sandwich tasted well deserved.

Leif had had the idea to clean out the old pigpen. The goal was to throw out decades of accumulated junk and install shelving so that anyone who needed to find a certain-sized screw or hammer could do so easily. The last time the pigpen had held any pigs was in the 1950s. We emptied generations of junk—knacks, tools, parts, pipes, and buckets—onto the lawn so we could decide what we'd haul to the dump.

That's when we realized the foundation of the 150-year-old building had completely crumbled. The floorboards had rotted away. The support beams were sawdust. Gavin sucked down a cigarette as Leif said resignedly, "Ahh, man!" We ripped up the floorboards and support beams until night came and it was too dark to see.

The next morning, we got up early. The foundation that held the beams in place had corroded, and we would need to pour concrete. Leif, Gavin, and I piled into Leif's truck and drove to the closest home-improvement store. We bought an eighty-pound bag of cement. By the time we were back at the farm, my father had lined the foundation with boards. He asked how many bags we'd bought. When we told him one, he sent Leif back to buy eight more. This was going to take awhile.

We mixed and poured concrete, then cut new support beams and floorboards from the lumber that had been drying in the barn since our grandfather placed it there in stacks, decades ago. It was all red and white oak that had grown in the woods surrounding the farm—enough lumber to replace the floorboards in every single building on the property. My father guessed the value of the wood for the new foundation to be several thousand dollars.

We took a long break at lunch to eat bologna sandwiches with steaming bowls of tomato soup. It felt good to work together to fix what was in disrepair. We could finish only half the job: the rest would have to wait until spring. The lumber would be waiting for us.

THE FOLLOWING WEEKEND, I got a call from Uncle Lowell, my father's youngest brother and the family's only hunter, asking if I'd like to join him at the farm. I was curious and a little nervous when I met Lowell outside the farmhouse just before sunset on a frigid November evening.

He didn't say a word, only waved for me to follow him to the edge of the woods. He walked through the leaves, barely making a sound. I tried to be equally quiet, but twigs cracked and leaves rustled at my every step. I winced with each shuffle, until Lowell stopped suddenly in the shadow of an oak and stared into the sloping, recently mown field.

We stood side by side and waited in complete silence. As the sun went down, my toes grew cold. The late-fall wind was sharp on my ears. In the field, an apple fell from an old tree with a thud. The wind shifted from west to northwest, sounding like an uneasy ocean through the few remaining leaf-lined branches.

We became part of the woods. My senses grew acute. I could hear the faintest creaks and cracks of the trees as they cooled in the evening. In the dimming light, colors seemed more vibrant. I began to notice things I'd never sensed before. First, close by, the sweet smell of recently fallen acorns, then oyster mushrooms, light gray and neatly shelved on an old stump a few feet away. When the wind puffed, a faint scent of aging wild grass filled my head.

Lowell slowly raised his right arm and pointed to the far end of the field, where a proud buck had trotted out from a line of yews. Then he raised his left arm and pointed directly in front of us, where three does grazed in the field. They had appeared so quickly that I wondered whether they had been there the whole time. It was as if we had become invisible to the deer, while they became visible to us.

The buck approached the does until he was standing directly in front of us. Lowell raised his rifle, and I raised mine. We aimed. My shot broke the evening silence—and missed the buck completely. The four deer stared at us curiously, as if we, too, had appeared from nowhere. I frantically pulled back the bolt of the rifle and pushed it forward to reload. In the cold, I was pouring sweat. Scared, flushed, and shaken, I raised the rifle to my shoulder. We both fired. The buck jumped, ran forward ten feet, and fell dead. The does ran into the woods. My shoulders were in knots. I could no longer feel my toes. Lowell glanced at me. "Let's warm up for a minute," he said. "You've got some work ahead of you."

Lowell insists that I shot the deer. But I suspect his purpose was to instill in me the biggest lesson in hunting: the responsibility a hunter carries for taking life. Field dressing a deer—an apprentice's albatross—is not pretty. You make an incision in the abdomen, through which you pull the warm, steaming intestines, stomach, and organs. The blood makes everything slimy. The heat, blood, and smell, while you are literally up to your elbows in deer, is enough to make even the most grizzled meat eater consider vegetarianism.

I took extra-special care when I cooked that deer, and every animal since. I've also improved my aim.

Lebanon Bologna Sandwiches makes 2 sandwiches

Lebanon bologna is a sliced sandwich meat commonly found in southeastern Pennsylvania. It comes in several forms—the most common are original and sweet. The original version is quite similar to salami in taste and texture, but the sweet version (the kind my grandfather used to make this sandwich) is unique. In addition to being cured, smoked, and fermented, the sweet bologna rounds out those complex flavors to make a balanced forcemeat. Sweet and sour is a common flavor play in Pennsylvania Dutch cuisine, and Lebanon bologna is a good example. My favorite brand is Seltzer's. If you ever find it at your grocery store, pick some up and be ready for a whole new taste. If you can't get it locally, you can order it online from seltzersbologna.com.

2 tablespoons salted butter, at
  room temperature

4 slices white bread

8 slices sweet Lebanon bologna
  (see headnote)

1 cup torn iceberg lettuce

Spread the butter over the bread, then make sandwiches using the bologna and lettuce. Serve.

The Best Meat Loaf serves 6 to 8

I wrote a variation of this recipe for *Gourmet* when I worked in the test kitchens. Since then, I've made a few tweaks over the years, adding more onion, garlic, and herbs and dropping the spices. There are several secrets to its success and popularity. First, instead of laying strips of bacon over the top, I've blended them into the meat-loaf mix, along with prunes, which bring a subtle sweetness to the flavor. A high proportion of bread crumbs adds plenty of lightness, and the meat loaf is baked without a loaf pan, which gives it a brown and flavorful crust. Those little touches, along with a healthy dose of Worcestershire sauce and a dab of vinegar, make this meat loaf my new standard. Garlic-Roasted Brussels Chips (page 211) make for a crunchy and unusual garnish. Save a few slices for leftover sandwiches; you won't be sorry.

1 cup coarsely ground fresh bread crumbs (from white bread)

⅓ cup milk

2 medium onions

5 garlic cloves

1 celery stalk

1 carrot

2 tablespoons unsalted butter or Master Fat (page 23)

3 tablespoons Worcestershire sauce

1 tablespoon cider vinegar

1 tablespoon kosher salt

1½ teaspoons black pepper

4 ounces bacon

½ cup pitted prunes

2 pounds meat loaf mix (equal parts ground pork, veal, and beef)

2 large eggs

½ cup chopped mixed fresh herbs (parsley, sage, thyme, basil)

Preheat the oven to 350°F.

Soak the bread crumbs in the milk in a large bowl. Coarsely chop the onions, garlic, celery, and carrot, then pulse them together in the food processor until they are finely chopped.

Heat the butter in a large heavy skillet over medium heat until hot. Add the finely chopped vegetables (don't clean the food processor) and cook, stirring occasionally, until they are tender, 8 to 10 minutes. Add the vegetables to the bread crumbs, along with the Worcestershire, vinegar, salt, and pepper.

Pulse the bacon and prunes in the food processor until they are finely chopped, then add to the bowl with the vegetables. Add the meat loaf mix, eggs, and herbs and mix everything together with your hands. Form the meat loaf into a 9-by-5-inch oval and place it in a 13-by-9-inch baking dish.

Bake the meat loaf until it is cooked through (an instant-read thermometer will register 155°F), about 1¼ hours. Let the meat loaf stand for 10 minutes before serving.

Rabbit in Cider-Mustard Sauce serves 4 to 6

In the last few years, I've seen rabbit at more and more supermarkets, thanks largely to Ariane Daguin, who owns D'Artagnan, which supplies top-quality meats and other edible goodies all over the country. Rabbit is easy to cook and downright delicious. Of course, if you're a hunter, then you'll know where to get your own supply.

This recipe builds on the classic dish of rabbit in mustard sauce by adding fresh, sweet apple cider to balance the tang of the mustard. By the way, this recipe also works well with chicken.

1 (2½- to 3-pound) rabbit

2 tablespoons extra-virgin olive oil or Master Fat (page 23)

Kosher salt and black pepper

1 large onion, chopped

4 garlic cloves, finely chopped

1 cup dry white wine

1 cup apple cider

⅓ cup Dijon mustard

2 tablespoons unsalted butter

1 tablespoon chopped fresh dill

Cut the rabbit into serving pieces: front legs, hind legs, and torso (which includes the flap meat, my favorite part).

Heat the oil in a large heavy pot over medium-high heat until it shimmers. Pat the rabbit dry, then sprinkle with 1 teaspoon salt and ¾ teaspoon pepper. Brown the rabbit, in batches if necessary, about 6 minutes per batch. Transfer the rabbit to a plate.

Add the onion and garlic to the pot and cook, stirring occasionally, until the onion is browned, 6 to 8 minutes. Return the rabbit to the pot, along with any juices from the plate, and add the wine and cider. Cover the pot and simmer over low heat until the rabbit is very tender, 1¼ to 1½ hours. Transfer the rabbit to a serving dish and increase the heat to a boil. Boil the braising liquid until it is reduced by half, 8 to 10 minutes. Remove the pot from the heat and whisk in the mustard, then the butter and dill, and season with salt and pepper to taste. Pour the sauce over the rabbit and serve.

Mustard-Garlic Venison Roast (or Boneless Leg of Lamb) serves 4

The hind-leg muscles of a deer are well suited for roasts. There are several muscles on the leg, which includes the equivalents of the eye of round and top round in beef. If you cut crosswise through the leg to make steaks, you end up with a piece of meat with several different muscles in it, and each muscle cooks at a slightly different rate. That means that some bites will be overcooked and chewy, while others won't be done quite enough. To avoid this, I like to detach each muscle and cook them separately to medium-rare in the center. The goal is to reach 130°F in the center of the roast, so I pull the roasts out of the oven when they are around 120°F and 125°F and then let them rest for at least 10 minutes. These muscles can be quite thick, so I use this recipe to get lots of flavor all through the meat.

This recipe also works for a boneless leg of lamb, which takes equally well to the heady flavors of mustard and garlic.

2 garlic cloves

Kosher salt

1½ tablespoons Dijon mustard

2 teaspoons finely chopped fresh rosemary

1 (2- to 2½-pound) venison hind-leg roast or boneless leg of lamb, trimmed of any silverskin

Black pepper

1 tablespoon extra-virgin olive oil or Master Fat (page 23)

1 cup veal stock, chicken stock, or low-sodium broth

1 tablespoon unsalted butter

Preheat the oven to 325°F.

Mince and mash the garlic and a pinch of salt to a paste with a chef's knife. Stir together the garlic paste, mustard, and rosemary.

Place the venison roast (smooth side down) on a work surface with the pointed (thinner) end nearest you. Starting at the top, make a lengthwise incision down the center of the roast, cutting two thirds of the way down through the meat (be careful not to cut all the way through). Using your fingers, pull open the roast slightly. Now butterfly it by turning your knife horizontally and slicing the roast open, first on one side, then on the other, so it opens and lies flat, being careful not to cut all the way through.

Season the roast all over with 1 teaspoon salt and ½ teaspoon pepper. Spread the mustard mixture evenly over the cut side of the roast. Roll the roast up on itself, then tie it with kitchen string.

Heat the oil in a large heavy ovenproof skillet until it shimmers. Place the roast in the skillet, then immediately transfer the skillet to the oven. Roast until an instant-read thermometer registers 120°F for medium-rare, 25 to 35 minutes. Transfer the roast to a cutting board and let it rest for at least 10 minutes.

Add the stock to the skillet, bring it to a boil, and let it reduce by half. Stir in any accumulated juices from the cutting board. Remove the skillet from the heat, whisk in the butter, and season with salt and pepper to taste.

Remove the string and slice the roast thinly crosswise. Serve with the pan sauce.

Venison Loin (or Beef Tenderloin) with Creamy Leek Sauce   serves 4

This recipe is easy, has great flavor (thanks to a secret ingredient added to the sauce—an anchovy fillet), and is an elegant way to show off a prized cut of venison. The Creamy Leek Sauce is a versatile sauce for your repertoire. You can serve it with just about anything from fish and chicken to pasta, even on a piece of toast. If you're not a hunter, beef tenderloin can easily be substituted for venison loin.

2 garlic cloves

Kosher salt

2 tablespoons finely chopped fresh rosemary

3 tablespoons extra-virgin olive oil

¾ teaspoon black pepper

1 (2-pound) venison loin or beef tenderloin, trimmed of any silverskin and halved

3 medium leeks, pale green and white parts only

2 tablespoons unsalted butter

1 anchovy fillet

1 cup chicken stock or low-sodium broth

1 cup heavy cream

Preheat the oven to 350°F.

Mince and mash the garlic and ¼ teaspoon salt to a paste with a chef's knife, then stir together with the rosemary, 2 tablespoons of the oil, 1 teaspoon salt, and ½ teaspoon of the pepper. Rub the marinade all over the meat. Cook immediately or marinate for up to 2 hours.

Slice the leeks crosswise and rinse under cold running water. Heat the butter in a large heavy skillet until it is hot. Add the leeks, ½ teaspoon salt, and the remaining ¼ teaspoon pepper. Cover the skillet and cook, stirring, over medium heat until the leeks are tender, about 8 minutes. Uncover the skillet, then add the anchovy fillet and the chicken stock. Bring the liquid to a boil and reduce until it is almost completely evaporated, 6 to 10 minutes. Add the cream and bring to a boil. Reduce the sauce until it is slightly thickened, about 5 minutes. Keep the sauce warm.

Heat the remaining 1 tablespoon oil in a large heavy oven-proof skillet over medium heat until it shimmers. Sear the meat on one side until browned, about 4 minutes. Turn the meat over and transfer the skillet to the oven. Roast the loin until medium-rare (110°F; the temperature will rise as the meat rests), 8 to 10 minutes. Transfer the meat to a cutting board and let it rest for 10 minutes. Slice the meat and sprinkle with salt to taste. Serve with the leek sauce.

Venison Loin with Apple-Shallot Hash serves 4

One recent fall, after a summer full of heavy rains, I was at the farm, deer hunting with my friend Steve. It was unseasonably warm for late fall, and there were still a few sweet apples clinging to the branches of the trees. Steve, who grew up hunting on the eastern shore of Chesapeake Bay, is an avid hunter and expert skinner. As the sun was beginning to get low, he spotted a deer in the field. We whispered that the venison would make for a great meal, and I decided this would be the deer I would shoot that year.

The next evening, we dined on venison, paired with a sweet, late-season apple-shallot hash. Steve claimed it was the best venison meal he'd ever had.

2 garlic cloves

Kosher salt

2 tablespoons dried herbes de Provence

1 tablespoon Dijon mustard

2 tablespoons extra-virgin olive oil

½ teaspoon black pepper

1 (2-pound) venison loin, trimmed of any silverskin and halved

3 mixed apples (McIntosh, Gala, and/or Granny Smith)

½ stick unsalted butter

3 medium shallots, finely chopped

1 tablespoon finely chopped fresh sage

½ cup apple cider

2 teaspoons apple cider vinegar

½ teaspoon cornstarch

Preheat the oven to 350°F.

Mince and mash the garlic and ¼ teaspoon salt to a paste with a chef's knife. Stir together with the herbes de Provence, mustard, 1 tablespoon of the oil, 1 teaspoon salt, and the pepper. Rub the marinade all over the meat. Cook immediately or marinate for up to 2 hours.

Core the apples and cut them into ¼-inch dice. Heat the butter in a large heavy skillet over medium-high heat until hot. Add the shallots to the skillet and sauté until browned, about 8 minutes. Add the apples and sage and cook, stirring, until the apples just start to brown, about 5 minutes. Stir together the cider, vinegar, and cornstarch, then add to the skillet. Bring to a simmer, stirring, and simmer until thickened, 1 minute. Keep the hash warm.

Heat the remaining 1 tablespoon oil in a large heavy oven-proof skillet over medium heat until it shimmers. Sear the meat on one side until browned, about 4 minutes. Turn the meat over and transfer the skillet to the oven. Roast the loin until medium-rare (120°F; the temperature will rise as the meat rests), 8 to 10 minutes. Transfer the meat to a cutting board and let it rest for 10 minutes. Slice the meat and sprinkle with salt to taste. Serve with the apple-shallot hash.

Chunky Chipotle Venison (or Beef) Chili serves 8

This recipe is an Americanized chili (as opposed to the Roast Pork Chili on page 77 that uses dried Mexican chiles as its flavor base). The beauty to this recipe, aside from the fact that it's absolutely delicious and satisfying, is that there are no hard-to-find ingredients required. Everything (except the deer) can be purchased at your local supermarket. If you're not a hunter, simply substitute beef chuck or pork butt for the venison and get cookin'.

8 ounces bacon, chopped

4 pounds venison shoulder and/ or neck meat or beef chuck, cut into 1- to 1½-inch chunks

Kosher salt and black pepper

3 medium onions, chopped

2 red bell peppers, chopped

6 garlic cloves, finely chopped

2 tablespoons paprika

1 tablespoon ground cumin

2 tablespoons dried oregano, crumbled

1 bay leaf

2 (28- to 32-ounce) cans whole peeled tomatoes in juice

2–3 tablespoons chopped chipotle chiles in adobo

1 (15- to 16-ounce) can kidney beans, rinsed and drained

Accompaniments

Diced white onion, shredded cheddar cheese, sour cream, tortilla chips, chopped cilantro

Cook the bacon in a 6- to 8-quart heavy pot over medium heat, stirring occasionally, until browned, 6 to 8 minutes. Transfer the bacon with a slotted spoon to paper towels to drain. Season the venison with 2½ teaspoons salt and 1 teaspoon pepper. Increase the heat to medium-high and brown the venison in the bacon fat in the pot, in batches, transferring the venison to a plate as it is browned, about 6 minutes per batch.

Pour off all but 3 tablespoons of the fat from the pot. Add the onions, bell peppers, and garlic and sauté, stirring occasionally, until they begin to brown, 8 to 10 minutes. Stir in the paprika and cumin and sauté until fragrant, about 1 minute. Return the venison to the pot, along with any juices accumulated on the plate. Stir in the oregano, bay leaf, tomatoes with juice, and chipotles. Bring the liquid to a simmer and cover the pot. Braise over low heat, simmering, until the venison is very tender, 3½ to 4 hours. Uncover the pot, bring to a boil, and boil until the chili is slightly thickened, 15 to 20 minutes. Skim off any fat, if desired. Stir in the beans, season with salt and pepper to taste, and remove the bay leaf. Sprinkle with the reserved bacon.

Serve the chili with the diced onion, shredded cheese, sour cream, chips, and cilantro.

Mushroom Venison (or Beef) Stew serves 6

If you're a hunter, or you know a hunter, you're always looking for good venison recipes to cook those not-so-tender parts of the deer. The front legs, torso, and neck meat are all very flavorful, but they are nearly fatless, well-exercised muscles. The answer to coaxing that meat into an unctuous meal is braising. This recipe features mushrooms and apple, which, fittingly, are staples of the deer's diet. The deep, woodsy flavors of the mushrooms and the slight sweetness of the apple pair well with the meat. The result is a sophisticated stew worthy of the most discerning palates.

The dish is made to be served with Red Cabbage Balsamic Slaw with Bacon Bits and Parsley (page 220) and Roasted Garlic and Rosemary Polenta (page 196) or boiled egg noodles. Garlic-Roasted Brussels Chips (page 211) make a crunchy garnish, too. If you don't have venison and want to make this wonderful fall stew, use beef chuck.

½ ounce dried porcini mushrooms

2 pounds venison shoulder, torso, or neck meat or beef chuck

Kosher salt and black pepper

3 tablespoons Master Fat (page 23) or extra-virgin olive oil

3 medium shallots, finely chopped

1 pound mixed fresh wild mushrooms

4 garlic cloves, minced

1 carrot, finely chopped

1 celery stalk, finely chopped

1 Granny Smith apple, peeled, cored, and finely chopped

1 cup dry red wine

2 cups veal stock, chicken stock, or low-sodium broth

½ stick unsalted butter

2 tablespoons Worcestershire sauce

1 bay leaf

2 tablespoons finely chopped fresh dill

Grind the porcini to a powder in a spice grinder and set aside. Remove any silverskin from the venison, then cut the meat into 1-inch pieces. Season the meat with 2 teaspoons salt and ¾ teaspoon pepper.

Heat the fat in a large heavy pot over medium-high heat until it shimmers. Brown the meat in batches, 6 to 8 minutes per batch. Transfer the venison to a plate.

Add the shallots to the pot and cook, stirring occasionally, until browned, about 6 minutes. Add the fresh mushrooms and garlic and cook until any liquid given off by the mushrooms has evaporated and they begin to brown, about 8 minutes. Add the carrot, celery, and apple and cook, stirring occasionally, until the vegetables are softened, about 6 minutes. Add the red wine and boil until the liquid is reduced by half, about 3 minutes. Return the venison to the pot, along with any juices from the plate, and add the stock, butter, Worcestershire, bay leaf, and porcini powder. Bring the stew to a simmer over medium-low heat. Cover the pot and cook until the venison is tender and falling apart, 3 to 4 hours.

Season the stew with salt and pepper to taste, and remove the bay leaf. Stir in the dill and serve.

Groundhog (or Chicken or Rabbit) Cacciatore   serves 6

All the lettuce . . . was . . . gone. So were the cauliflower and all the soybeans. This could only be the work of one thing: a groundhog. During the spring, several holes had been dug under the garden fence. I tried to fill them with rocks and dirt, but to no avail. Once my vegetables started vanishing, I knew there was only one solution. On an afternoon — a tranquil one — the greedy, well-fed groundhog popped its head up to scope out the garden's offerings. I shot him dead. Then I felt terrible. He was so cute, and really, who doesn't love fresh vegetables for lunch? I made up my mind to cook him instead of letting him waste away in the field.

Groundhog meat is very much like rabbit, so I put the meat to use in a cacciatore, the tomato-based Italian hunters' stew. This recipe works just as well with rabbit or chicken and is completely comforting when served with Roasted Garlic and Rosemary Polenta (page 196).

1 groundhog, skinned, gutted, and quartered, or chicken or rabbit, quartered

Kosher salt and black pepper

3 tablespoons extra-virgin olive oil

1 medium onion, chopped

2 carrots, chopped

4 garlic cloves, minced

1 cup dry white wine

2 pounds tomatoes, chopped, or 1 (28-ounce) can whole tomatoes in juice

3 tablespoons chopped brined capers

2 strips fresh orange zest

2 anchovy fillets

1 bay leaf

2 tablespoons unsalted butter

Remove the grayish glands from underneath the groundhog's front legs (you may have to cut into the meat to find them). Pat the meat dry and season with 1 teaspoon salt and ¾ teaspoon pepper. Heat the oil in a large heavy pot over medium-high heat until it shimmers. Brown the meat well on both sides, in batches if necessary, about 6 minutes per batch. Transfer to a plate.

Add the onion, carrots, and garlic to the pot and cook until the vegetables are browned, 8 to 10 minutes. Add the wine and boil until the liquid is reduced by half, about 5 minutes. Stir in the tomatoes, capers, orange zest, anchovies, and bay leaf, then nestle the meat into the sauce. Reduce the heat and simmer, covered, until the meat is tender, 1½ to 2 hours.

When the meat is tender, remove it from the pot, leaving the sauce in the pot. Simmer the sauce until it is slightly thickened, about 10 minutes. Stir in the butter. Season the sauce with salt and pepper to taste, remove the bay leaf, and return the meat to the pot. Serve in shallow bowls.

Crispy Potato Cake with Garlic and Herbs serves 8

These potatoes are cooked in a large skillet before being finished in the oven. The result is a crisp potato crust and a creamy, garlicky inside. I like to cut the cake into wedges and serve it on the plate with Rabbit in Cider-Mustard Sauce (page 186) or Mustard-Garlic Venison Roast (or Boneless Leg of Lamb) (page 186) or as a side for Garlic-Pesto Roast Chicken (page 55).

¾ stick unsalted butter, melted

2½ pounds baking potatoes

2 garlic cloves, finely chopped

¼ cup mixed finely chopped fresh herbs (thyme, rosemary, marjoram, oregano), plus more for sprinkling

Kosher salt and black pepper

Preheat the oven to 425°F.

Brush a 10-inch cast-iron or ovenproof nonstick skillet with some of the melted butter. Peel the potatoes, then thinly slice them, using an adjustable slicer or a very sharp knife. Layer one third of the potatoes in the skillet, overlapping the slices, and drizzle them with some of the butter. Sprinkle the potato layer with one third each of the garlic and herbs and sprinkle with ½ teaspoon each salt and pepper. Layer half of the remaining potatoes over the first layer, then drizzle them with half of the remaining butter. Sprinkle with half of the remaining garlic and herbs and ½ teaspoon each salt and pepper. Layer the remaining potatoes on top and drizzle the remaining butter over the potatoes. Sprinkle with the remaining garlic and herbs and ½ teaspoon each salt and pepper.

Cook the potato cake over medium heat until the bottom is pale golden, about 6 minutes. Cover the skillet and transfer to the oven. Bake until the potato cake is very soft, about 30 minutes. Let the cake cool for 10 minutes in the pan, then carefully invert it onto a serving platter or a cutting board. Serve sliced into wedges, sprinkled with more herbs.

Celery Root and Parsnip Puree   serves 6

These two roots were meant to be together. Both parsnip and celery root have a slight sweetness to them and are hearty enough to last all winter. Pureeing the cooked veggies in a food processor gives you a coarser, rustic texture, while blending them makes for an elegant, silky smooth puree. Either way, you'll have a side dish that puts regular mashed potatoes to shame.

1½ pounds celery root

8 ounces parsnips

⅔ cup heavy cream

2 tablespoons unsalted butter

Kosher salt and black pepper

Remove and discard the root end of the celery root, then peel the celery root and cut it into 1-inch pieces. Peel and core the parsnips, then cut into 1-inch pieces. Place the celery root and parsnips in a steamer basket set over a pot of boiling water and cover the pot. Steam the vegetables until they are very tender, 15 to 20 minutes.

Transfer the vegetables to a food processor or blender and add the cream, butter, ¾ teaspoon salt, and ½ teaspoon pepper. Pulse until very smooth, about 1 minute. Season with salt and pepper to taste and serve.

Roasted Garlic and Rosemary Polenta serves 4

Every cook needs a polenta recipe, and this one always surprises with its huge flavor. The secret to this killer version: an entire head of roasted garlic. It pairs perfectly with Rabbit in Cider-Mustard Sauce (page 186) or Mushroom Venison (or Beef) Stew (page 192).

2 cups chicken stock or low-sodium broth

1 cup water

1 cup cornmeal

1 head roasted garlic (see page 78)

1 teaspoon finely chopped fresh rosemary

Kosher salt and black pepper

½ cup mascarpone cheese

Bring the stock and water to a boil in a heavy medium saucepan over medium heat. Whisk in the cornmeal in a slow stream. Squeeze the garlic cloves from their skins, then add to the polenta, along with the rosemary and ½ teaspoon each salt and pepper.

Cook the polenta, whisking occasionally at first and more frequently toward the end of cooking, until it is thickened and soft to the chew, 45 minutes to an hour, depending on the grind of your cornmeal. Whisk in the mascarpone, season with salt and pepper to taste, and serve.

Grandmom's Bread makes one 9-by-4-inch loaf

My grandmother always made her own bread, and her recipe has been passed down to me. This style of bread baking has its roots firmly planted in the Eastern United States of yesteryear. There is a low proportion of liquid to flour, and the liquid is milk, which adds sweetness and a light texture to the bread. The dough is baked in a loaf pan so that the bread can be sliced for sandwiches.

These days we find French- or Italian-style bread at almost every bakery and grocery store, but there was a time (not so long ago) when bread like my grandmother's was the only sort available. I use this recipe for sandwiches, and My Bread (page 200) for baguettes and rustic loaves. They are both wonderful.

1½ teaspoons active dry yeast

2 tablespoons warm water

1 cup whole milk, scalded and cooled

3 cups all-purpose flour

1 tablespoon sugar

1 teaspoon kosher salt

1 tablespoon melted shortening

Soften the yeast in the warm water in a small bowl. Place the milk and the yeast mixture in the bowl of a stand mixer. Add 2 cups of the flour, the sugar, and salt and mix until combined. Add the shortening and mix to combine. Turn the dough out onto a lightly floured work surface and gradually add the remaining 1 cup flour, kneading the dough until it is smooth and elastic, about 6 minutes. (If you don't have a stand mixer, you can make the dough by hand. Place the ingredients in a bowl and stir with a wooden spoon until combined well.)

Generously grease the bowl, then add the dough, turning it to grease it all over, and cover the bowl with a kitchen towel. Let the dough rise until it has doubled in bulk, 1 to 1½ hours.

Fold the dough over on itself, cover, and let it rise again until it has doubled in bulk, 40 to 45 minutes.

Grease a 9-by-4-inch loaf pan.

Turn the dough out onto a lightly floured work surface and form into a ball. Let the dough rest for 10 minutes, then shape it into a loaf and place the loaf in the loaf pan. Let the dough rise, covered with a kitchen towel, until it has doubled in bulk, about 1 hour.

Meanwhile, preheat the oven to 400°F, with a rack in the middle. Bake the bread until it is golden on top and sounds hollow when tapped, about 50 minutes. Let the bread cool slightly in the pan before turning it out and cooling completely on a rack.

Cloud Biscuits makes about 12 biscuits

The secret to the cloud-like texture of these classic American biscuits is the shortening that is used instead of butter. You can spread butter over the warm biscuits after they're baked, along with Strawberry-Cherry-Rhubarb Preserves (page 152). This recipe is from my grandmother's kitchen and is very versatile. The method instructs you to pat out and cut out the biscuits, but if you prefer a more rustic drop biscuit, see the variation.

2 cups all-purpose flour

1 tablespoon sugar

4 teaspoons baking powder

½ teaspoon kosher salt

½ cup cold shortening

⅔ cup whole milk

1 large egg

Preheat the oven to 450°F, with a rack in the upper third.

Stir together the flour, sugar, baking powder, and salt in a large bowl. Cut in the shortening with your hands until mostly combined, with some small lumps of shortening remaining. Whisk together the milk and egg in a small bowl, then add to the dry ingredients all at once. Using a fork, stir the dough together until it follows the fork around the bowl. Let the dough stand for 10 minutes, then transfer the dough to a heavily floured work surface and dust the top of the dough well with flour. Pat the dough gently into a ¾-inch-thick disk. Cut out 2-inch rounds, patting out the dough once more.

Bake the biscuits on an ungreased baking sheet until golden, 12 to 15 minutes.

Variation: Drop Biscuits

Increase the milk to ¾ cup and, instead of patting and cutting, just mix and drop the biscuits onto the baking sheet.

My Bread   makes 1 loaf

I love baking bread, and I learned the basics of this recipe from Richard Bertinet, a great baker and teacher, when I visited his baking school in Bath, England. I've learned many techniques from Richard that make for beautiful loaves. One is to add water to the oven (in the form of a mist or an ice cube). The moist environment helps form a crisp crust. This dough will seem very wet to you if you're used to American-style dough (like my grandmother's on page 197). It has much more liquid in it than most home bakers are used to seeing, but the extra water produces a very crisp crust and a moist loaf. If you have a kitchen scale (they're cheap and make everything easier), measure the flour and water by weight for a more accurate recipe. If not, you can use the cup measurements.

This style is reminiscent of the western European rustic breads that have become popular in recent years. It's perfect for crostini and also wonderful when dipped in olive oil.

1 teaspoon active dry yeast

1¾ cups (400 grams) warm water

4¼ cups (500 grams) all-purpose or bread flour

1 teaspoon kosher salt

Place the yeast and water in the bowl of a stand mixer. Add the flour and salt and mix on low speed with the paddle attachment until combined. Increase the speed and beat the dough until it no longer sticks to the side of the bowl, about 3 minutes. Turn the dough out onto a lightly floured work surface and form into a ball. Lightly flour the bowl and place the dough back in the bowl. Cover the bowl with a kitchen towel and let the dough rise until it has doubled in bulk, 1 to 1½ hours.

Turn the dough out onto a lightly floured work surface, form into a rough oval, and place on the baking sheet. Dust the top of the loaf with flour, then loosely cover with a kitchen towel. Let the dough rise until it has doubled in bulk, about 45 minutes.

Meanwhile, preheat the oven to 500°F, with a rack in the middle. Generously flour a baking sheet.

Make 3 cuts in the top of the loaf with a razor blade or a very sharp knife and place the baking sheet in the oven. Place an ice cube in the bottom of the oven (or spray the oven with a water-filled atomizer). Bake until the bread is golden brown and sounds hollow when tapped, about 1 hour. Transfer the bread to a rack to cool completely.

Black Walnut Cake   serves 8

My grandmother came up with ways to use all of the black walnuts we get at the farm, where the trees grow like weeds. They're literally tough nuts to crack (my grandfather would drive over them with his tractor). Regular English walnuts are a less labor-intensive and milder substitute. My Aunt Janet sent me a copy of my grandmother's original handwritten recipe, which I've modified only slightly. This is a dense cake and doesn't need a frosting, but a scoop of ice cream makes it even better.

2 cups all-purpose flour

½ cup black or English walnut pieces

1¼ teaspoons baking soda

1 teaspoon kosher salt

2 sticks unsalted butter, at room temperature

1½ cups sugar

2 large eggs

1 teaspoon vanilla

1⅓ cups buttermilk

Preheat the oven to 350°F, with a rack in the middle. Butter and flour a 9-inch-square cake pan.

Whisk together the flour, walnuts, baking soda, and salt in a medium bowl.

Beat together the butter and sugar with an electric mixer until pale and fluffy, about 4 minutes. Add the eggs one at a time, beating well after each addition, then beat in the vanilla. Add the flour mixture and the buttermilk alternately in batches, beginning and ending with the flour mixture and mixing until just combined.

Pour the batter into the cake pan and smooth the top. Bake until a wooden toothpick inserted in the center comes out clean, 45 to 55 minutes. Cool in the pan on a rack for 1 hour. Invert the cake over a cake plate and serve.

Mincemeat Pie makes one 9-inch pie

(makes enough filling for four 9-inch pies)

This pie has been served at our Thanksgiving and Christmas tables for generations. I remember sitting on my father's lap as a young boy, tasting a bite of his slice (which was always drowned in rum) and feeling surprised that I liked it so much. Although it used to be common to put ground beef in your dessert, mincemeat has fallen out of fashion in this country, which is too bad, because it's delicious.

My grandmother's recipe is written loosely. At one point, it instructs you to add enough liquid to total 6 to 8 cups—any combination of "tangy" cider, orange juice, pineapple juice, lemon juice, corn syrup, dry wine, vinegar, honey, or molasses. I've come up with a combination that is balanced and reminds me of her version. My father approves, which gives me confidence that I'm on the right track. This recipe makes enough filling for four 9-inch pies, and it freezes particularly well. After you've made 1 pie, divide the remaining filling into 3 quarts. Freeze each quart of filling separately and thaw and reheat when you're ready to use it.

For the pastry dough

1¼ cups all-purpose flour

1 teaspoon light brown sugar

½ teaspoon kosher salt

1 stick unsalted butter, cut into cubes

2–3 tablespoons cold water

For the mincemeat

3 pounds ground beef (or beef and pork mixed)

8 ounces ground suet

2 pounds raisins

2 pounds dried currants

2 tablespoons finely grated orange zest

1 tablespoon finely grated lemon zest

8 apples (2½ quarts), chopped

1 cup dark brown sugar

1 cup sugar

2 teaspoons kosher salt

4 teaspoons ground cinnamon

2 teaspoons freshly grated nutmeg

2 teaspoons ground allspice

2 teaspoons ground ginger

1 teaspoon ground cloves

2 cups apple cider

1 cup orange juice

1 cup pineapple juice

1 cup dry white wine

½ cup apple cider vinegar or distilled white vinegar

½ cup honey

½ cup molasses

½ stick unsalted butter

Dark rum for serving

Vanilla ice cream for serving

Make the pastry dough: Work together the flour, brown sugar, salt, and butter with your hands until mostly combined, with some small lumps of butter remaining. Stir in 2 tablespoons of the water with a fork. Press a small handful of dough together; if it looks powdery and does not come together, stir in the remaining 1 tablespoon water. Transfer the dough to a sheet of plastic wrap. Using the edge of the plastic, fold the dough over onto itself, pressing until it comes together. Form the dough into a disk, wrap completely in the plastic, and chill for 1 hour.

Preheat the oven to 400°F, with a rack in the middle.

Roll out the pastry dough on a well-floured surface with a floured rolling pin into an 11-inch round. Place the dough in a 9-inch pie tin and crimp the edges. Place a sheet of parchment paper or foil over the dough, then fill with pie weights or dried beans. Bake the crust until it is set, about 25 minutes. Remove the parchment paper and the pie weights, then continue to bake the crust until it is golden, 10 to 15 minutes more. Let the pie shell cool to room temperature before filling.

Meanwhile, make the mincemeat: Brown the meat and suet, stirring occasionally, in a large heavy skillet (preferably cast-iron) over medium-high heat, about 10 minutes. Transfer the meat with a slotted spoon to a large heavy pot.

Add the remaining mincemeat ingredients with the beef and bring to a boil. Reduce the heat to a simmer and cook until the liquid has reduced and the filling is thickened, about 1¼ hours. Let the filling cool to warm, then spoon one quarter of the filling into the pie shell. (The remaining filling can be frozen in gallon airlock bags for up to 6 months; see headnote.) Serve the pie with dark rum poured over it and vanilla ice cream.

Apple and Concord Grape Tart serves 6 to 8

Several years ago, I planted grapevines at the farm, and I'm still waiting for a large harvest. Each year I end up with only a few clusters—not enough to make wine, but just enough for this dessert. There is a seasonal window, somewhere between late September and early October, during which the grapes and the apples are both ripe at the same time. They complement each other perfectly. This is the right end to any fall meal.

For the pastry dough

1¼ cups all-purpose flour

1 stick unsalted butter, cut into cubes

1 teaspoon light or dark brown sugar

½ teaspoon kosher salt

2–3 tablespoons cold water

For the filling

½ cup light brown sugar

2 teaspoons finely grated orange zest

¼ cup orange juice

½ teaspoon ground cinnamon

¼ teaspoon freshly grated nutmeg

¼ teaspoon kosher salt

5 Gala or McIntosh apples

½ cup Concord grapes

Make the pastry dough: Work together the flour, butter, brown sugar, and salt with your hands until mostly combined, with some small lumps of butter remaining. Stir in 2 tablespoons of the water with a fork. Press a small handful of dough together; if it looks powdery and does not come together, stir in the remaining 1 tablespoon water. Transfer the dough to a sheet of plastic wrap. Using the edge of the plastic, fold the dough over onto itself, pressing until it comes together. Form the dough into a disk, wrap completely in the plastic, and refrigerate for 1 hour.

Make the filling: Whisk together the brown sugar, orange zest, juice, cinnamon, nutmeg, and salt in a large bowl. Peel and core the apples, then slice them and add to the sugar mixture. Cut the grapes in half, remove the seeds, then toss them with the apples.

Preheat the oven to 425°F, with a rack in the middle.

On a well-floured surface, roll out the pastry dough with a floured rolling pin into a 13-by-9-inch rectangle. Transfer the dough to a 12-by-8½-inch baking sheet and crimp the edges. Pour the filling onto the dough, spreading evenly.

Bake the tart until the crust is golden, the filling is bubbling, and the apples have started to brown, about 45 minutes. Cool the tart slightly on a rack. Serve warm or at room temperature.

Fifty Heads of Garlic

ONE WARM MONDAY AFTERNOON in early November, my sister Cecily, our friend Steve, and I sat on the lawn, each drinking a beer. We deserved them: we had just finished tilling the entire garden by hand. For a full week after the tilling, my neck and back ached like they had never ached before. We used a pickax and an old hoe, which broke in half somewhere near the tomato patch in the middle of the garden. Steve had graciously volunteered to help us with the task. He, too, reveled in the quiet moment after the work, beer in hand. We sat, the three of us, in silence and stared at the work we'd finally finished.

Steve had unearthed a rusted buckle as he tilled near the butternut squash patch. He had picked it up and walked down the length of the garden to hand it to me, happy for the break from the labor. The buckle was an inch long and coated in what seemed like more than a hundred years of rust. The rust had chipped and corroded the metal so the buckle looked as though it were made of flaky pie dough or tightly wrapped phyllo. It might have belonged to a belt or a rifle strap: an anonymous relic of a generation long past. In its current state, it was unusable and unrestorable. I held it in my hand, thanked Steve, then slipped it into the pocket of my jeans.

As we sat in the grass and drank our beers, I brought the buckle from my pocket and felt it in my hand. I asked Cecily if she wanted to have the garden next year. She stared at me as if it were an absurd question. She said she'd never felt so grounded. Or did she use the words *close to the ground*? I can't remember, but she meant both of those things. She said she'd never eaten so well. We spoke about the food we'd eaten all summer and the people we'd shared it with. We spoke about our grandfather and his garden. She described a strawberry she remembered eating when she was ten, a memory so powerful and vivid, she could still taste the fruit.

I recalled a similar moment: my grandfather giving me a single strawberry that he held out in his seemingly enormous hand. I remember how warm it was from the sun and how sweet it was. I remember it exploding in my mouth with the flavor of summer. I remember the pop and crunch of the seeds.

I stood up and stretched my arms toward the fading afternoon sun. My back hurt. Cecily stood also, and together we walked to the far end of the garden, near the asparagus clump I had put there last spring. We dug long, shallow trenches with our hands and planted fifty cloves of garlic. Then we covered the cloves with the soft, freshly tilled earth. At the end of one of the garlic rows, I placed the buckle in the dirt. In the spring, we will till the garden again. I might find the buckle, or any number of other sentimental but otherwise useless treasures. What I know I will find are fifty heads of fresh spring garlic.

And for my birthday next spring, I'll buy myself a gas-powered tiller.

Cider-Braised Bacon Crostini with Fried Green Tomatoes and Parsley Salad serves 4

This recipe is the brainchild (stroke of genius might be a more appropriate phrase) of my friend Alan Sytsma, who spends many summer weekends with us at the farm. Alan had the idea to braise some bacon in apple cider that he had pressed with us at the farm. It quickly became his signature dish that he serves for Thanksgiving in his house. I've balanced that dish's rich sweetness with tart green tomatoes and a bright parsley salad.

1 pound slab bacon

1 cup apple cider

¼ cup whiskey

5 tablespoons extra-virgin olive oil

4 slices sourdough bread

4 scallions, trimmed

½ cup cornmeal

¼ teaspoon cayenne pepper

Kosher salt and black pepper

1 green tomato

1 cup fresh flat-leaf parsley leaves

1 tablespoon finely chopped shallot

1 tablespoon red wine vinegar or sherry vinegar

Preheat the oven to 350°F.

Trim any skin off the bacon and place it in a small baking dish. Pour the cider and whiskey over the bacon, then cover the dish tightly with foil. Braise it in the oven until the meaty part of the bacon is very tender, about 3½ hours. Remove the dish from the oven and let the bacon cool completely in the braising liquid. With a very sharp knife, cut the bacon into 4 slices and reserve until you're ready to serve the dish. (The bacon can be braised several days in advance and kept refrigerated.)

While the bacon braises, heat 2 tablespoons of the oil in a large heavy skillet over medium heat until it shimmers. Add the bread slices to the skillet and toast until both sides are well browned. Reserve the toasts.

Add 1 tablespoon of the remaining oil to the oil already in the skillet, then add the scallions. Cook the scallions over medium heat until they are browned and wilted, 4 to 6 minutes. Remove from the skillet and set aside. Do not clean the skillet.

Stir together the cornmeal, cayenne, and ½ teaspoon each salt and pepper on a small plate. Cut ¼-inch slices from the tomato. Place the slices on the cornmeal mixture, turning once or twice so the tomatoes are well coated. Add 1 tablespoon of the remaining oil to the oil already in the skillet and heat over medium heat until it shimmers.

Add the tomato slices and brown, turning once, 4 to 6 minutes total. Place 1 tomato slice on each toast, then divide the scallions among the tomato slices.

Add the bacon slices to the oil in the skillet and brown the bacon on both sides. Place 1 piece of the bacon on top of each crostini.

Toss the parsley leaves with the shallot, vinegar, the remaining 1 tablespoon oil, and a large pinch each salt and pepper. Top each crostini with some of the parsley salad and serve.

Garlic-Roasted Brussels Chips

serves 4 as a snack or side dish

Think you don't like Brussels sprouts? Think again. Everybody loves these crispy Brussels chips. These are one of my favorite fall snacks (you can serve them as a side dish for dinner, but you will have serious trouble making them last long enough to get to the table). They are also a great garnish for Mushroom Venison (or Beef) Stew (page 192) and The Best Meat Loaf (page 185), where they add a crispy crunch and a garlicky roasted flavor.

1 pound Brussels sprouts

2 garlic cloves, finely chopped

3 tablespoons extra-virgin olive oil

1 tablespoon unsalted butter, melted

¾ teaspoon kosher salt

½ teaspoon black pepper

Preheat the oven to 425°F, with a rack in the upper third. Line a baking sheet with aluminum foil.

Cut off and discard the bottoms of the sprouts so the outer leaves can be peeled away. Pull off the outer leaves and reserve. Thinly slice the sprouts crosswise. Toss the outer leaves and the sliced sprouts together with the garlic, oil, butter, salt, and pepper.

Spread the leaves and sprouts in one layer on the baking sheet. Bake until the leaves become browned and crisp, 10 to 16 minutes, checking frequently after 10 minutes. Remove the leaves as they crisp and transfer them to a serving bowl. Serve hot.

Pasta with Shredded Collard Greens   serves 4

In this method of cooking collard greens, the greens are rolled up tightly, like a cigar, then sliced crosswise paper-thin and cooked with olive oil and a lot of garlic in a very hot pan. It takes only a couple of minutes for the greens to wilt into tender piles of deliciousness. Prepared this way, the collards grace my table all fall and winter long, and tossed with a little bacon, toasted walnuts, and boiled macaroni, they become an ultrafast dinner. This technique works for all sorts of hearty greens, so feel free to experiment with Swiss chard, mustard greens, turnip greens, and the like.

4 slices bacon, chopped

½ cup walnut pieces

1 large bunch collard greens (about 1 pound)

3 tablespoons extra-virgin olive oil

4 garlic cloves, finely chopped

Kosher salt and black pepper

½ cup finely grated Parmigiano-Reggiano, plus more for the table

1 tablespoon apple cider vinegar

8 ounces elbow macaroni

Cook the bacon and walnuts in a large heavy skillet over medium heat, turning, until the bacon is crisp and the walnuts are golden, 6 to 8 minutes. Remove with a slotted spoon to a paper towel and let cool, then crumble the bacon. Do not clean the skillet.

Stack and roll up the collards tightly, like a cigar, then slice them as thinly as possible so they resemble Easter grass.

Add the oil to the skillet, along with the garlic. Cook, stirring, until the garlic is golden, 1 to 2 minutes. Add the collard greens and ¼ teaspoon each salt and pepper and cook over high heat, turning with tongs, until the collards are wilted, 3 to 4 minutes. Add the Parmesan and vinegar to the collards, along with the bacon and walnuts, then season with salt and pepper to taste.

Meanwhile, cook the pasta in heavily salted boiling water until it is al dente. Reserve ¼ cup of the pasta-cooking water, drain the pasta, and toss it with the collards, along with the reserved cooking water. Season with salt and pepper to taste and serve the pasta with additional Parmesan.

Escarole and Leek Pappardelle   serves 4 to 6

Leeks and escarole are fall and winter treats. Leeks contribute a deep, oniony sweetness to this dish, while escarole adds hearty green substance. Their combined flavors will have everyone slurping up the fat, creamy pappardelle.

1 (8-ounce) head escarole

2 large leeks, pale green and white parts only

2 tablespoons extra-virgin olive oil

1 tablespoon unsalted butter

Kosher salt and black pepper

½ cup heavy cream

8 ounces dried pappardelle

½ cup finely grated Parmigiano-Reggiano

Pinch of dried red pepper flakes

Bring a large pot of heavily salted water to a boil. Tear the escarole into large pieces and wash it well. Cook the escarole in the boiling water until tender, about 5 minutes. Remove the escarole from the water with tongs or a slotted spoon and transfer to a sieve. When it cools enough to handle, press on it to remove as much water as possible. Keep the water at a boil.

Halve the leeks lengthwise, then thinly slice them crosswise. Wash the leeks well. Cook the leeks in the oil and butter with 1 teaspoon salt and ½ teaspoon pepper in a large heavy skillet over medium heat until the leeks are golden, about 6 minutes. Add the escarole and cream to the skillet and boil until the liquid is slightly thickened, about 4 minutes.

Boil the pasta in the escarole water until it is al dente. Drain.

Toss the pasta with the escarole sauce, Parmesan, and pepper flakes. Season with salt and pepper to taste and serve.

Spinach and Walnut Lasagna serves 6 to 8

I often throw together a lasagna using a jar of summer tomatoes that we canned in August, but this version is extra-special. It uses a béchamel for the sauce and has layers of spinach that seem to melt into the noodles as the lasagna bubbles away in the oven. A layer of walnuts over the top adds crunch. Be sure to let the lasagna rest for the whole 15 minutes before you dive in, because the noodles continue to soak up liquid and flavor as it stands.

2½ pounds spinach

1 large onion, chopped

4 large garlic cloves, finely chopped

1¼ teaspoons kosher salt

¾ teaspoon black pepper

5 tablespoons extra-virgin olive oil

⅓ cup all-purpose flour

3½ cups whole milk

1 cup heavy cream

1 tablespoon dried oregano

½ teaspoon freshly grated nutmeg

½ cup finely grated Parmigiano-Reggiano

1 pound grated Monterey Jack cheese

12 (7-by-3-inch) no-boil lasagna sheets (about 7 ounces)

1 cup walnut pieces, toasted

Remove the coarse stems from the spinach and wash the leaves. Do not dry them. Place the spinach in a large heavy pot. Cover the pot and place it over medium-high heat. Steam the spinach, stirring once or twice, until it is soft, about 8 minutes. Transfer the spinach to a colander. When the spinach cools enough to handle, press out any remaining liquid, then chop.

Wipe out the pot. Cook the onion, garlic, salt, and pepper in the oil over medium-high heat until the onion is golden, about 10 minutes. Whisk in the flour and cook for 2 minutes. Whisk in the milk and the cream in a slow stream. Stir in the oregano and nutmeg. Bring the béchamel to a boil and cook, stirring occasionally, for 6 minutes. Remove the pot from the heat and stir in the Parmesan and half of the Monterey Jack.

Preheat the oven to 400°F.

Spread about 1 cup of the sauce over the bottom of a 13-by-9-inch broilerproof baking dish and place 3 noodles over the sauce, leaving a little space between each noodle. Spread another layer of sauce on top of the noodles, then top with half of the spinach. Make another layer of 3 noodles and sauce, then a layer of noodles, then sauce and the remaining spinach. Top with the remaining noodles and a final layer of sauce. Sprinkle the walnuts over the top, then the remaining Monterey Jack, and cover the pan with foil.

Bake the lasagna until it is bubbling, about 50 minutes. Uncover the pan and turn on the broiler. Broil the lasagna about 6 inches from the heat until the top is browned in spots, 6 to 8 minutes. Let the lasagna rest for 15 minutes before serving.

Potato-Cheddar Pancakes with Perfect Fried Eggs · serves 4

Frying an egg perfectly isn't difficult, but somehow it took me years to figure out. Now that I have, I get it right every time. I love crisp edges around the white, and a runny yolk. The trick is to start with a very hot pan to get the crisp whites and then reduce the heat and cover the skillet to cook the rest of the white through. Covering the skillet traps the heat inside and gently cooks the top of the egg, while keeping the bottom crisp. The beauty of this technique is that there's no need to flip the egg, so you don't risk breaking the yolk. The potato pancakes are a treat whether or not they're topped with eggs. A little cornstarch added to the mix makes them über-crunchy on the outside, and the chunks of cheddar inside are meltingly gooey. They're just the way to start a cold winter morning.

5 large eggs

2 (8-ounce) russet potatoes

1 medium onion

4 ounces sharp cheddar cheese, cut into small cubes

1 tablespoon cornstarch

Kosher salt and black pepper

4 tablespoons extra-virgin olive oil or Master Fat (page 23)

Beat 1 of the eggs in a medium bowl. Peel the potatoes, then grate them into the bowl using the large holes of a box grater. Grate the onion into the bowl. Toss the potato mixture with the cheese, cornstarch, 1 teaspoon salt, and ½ teaspoon pepper.

Heat 2 tablespoons of the oil in a large cast-iron or heavy nonstick skillet over medium heat until it shimmers. Divide the potato mixture into 4 mounds in the skillet, then flatten each mound into a patty. Cover the skillet and cook until the bottoms of the pancakes are golden and the edges are crisp. Flip the pancakes over and continue to cook, covered, until they are golden and crisp, about 10 minutes total. Transfer the pancakes to plates and wipe out the skillet.

Heat the remaining 2 tablespoons oil in the skillet over medium-high heat until very hot. Crack the remaining 4 eggs into the skillet and cook until the edges are crispy, about 3 minutes. Reduce the heat to very low, cover the skillet, and continue to cook until the whites are set but the yolks are still runny, about 2 minutes.

Top each potato pancake with a fried egg. Season with salt and pepper to taste and serve immediately.

Chicken with a Ton of Garlic   serves 4 to 6

I came up with this recipe after a long day in the garden. We had just planted what would become the following year's garlic, using the heads that we had saved from the previous summer. I was left with four heads of garlic and figured this was a great way to celebrate the coming crop. I used it all in this recipe, and the result is a beautiful ode to "the stinking rose."

Half of the garlic is roasted beforehand, mashed into a paste, and spread under the skin of the bird. The rest is stuffed inside the cavity, along with half a lemon and some thyme. The deep, caramelized flavor of the roasted garlic makes this taste like it's been on a rotisserie, but, in fact, it's just the oven.

2 heads roasted garlic (see page 78)

1 teaspoon fresh thyme leaves, plus 2 large fresh thyme sprigs

1 tablespoon extra-virgin olive oil

1¼ teaspoons kosher salt

1¼ teaspoons black pepper

1 (3½-pound) chicken

½ lemon

2 heads garlic, halved

Preheat the oven to 450°F, with a rack in the middle.

Peel and mash the roasted garlic together with the thyme leaves, oil, and ¼ teaspoon each salt and pepper.

Rinse the chicken and pat it dry. Being careful not to tear the skin, start at the large cavity and gently run your fingers between the skin and the meat to loosen the skin. Push the roasted garlic mixture under the skin, including around the thighs and drumsticks, and massage the skin from outside to spread the garlic evenly.

Squeeze the lemon half over the chicken, then season the chicken inside and out with the remaining 1 teaspoon each salt and pepper. Place the halved garlic heads, lemon half, and thyme sprigs in the cavity and loosely tie the legs together with kitchen string.

Roast the chicken until it is golden and the skin pulls away from the base of the drumsticks, about 50 minutes. Transfer the chicken to a cutting board and let it rest for 15 minutes before carving and serving.

Apple-Cider-Glazed Sticky Ribs serves 6 to 8

Fresh cider is perfect for adding flavorful, nuanced sweetness to a sophisticated version of sweet-and-sour barbecue sauce that goes on ribs as they finish cooking. A long oven-bake ensures tender meat, while the grill finish adds smoky caramelization. I originally made these ribs for a dinner to celebrate my cousin Leif's college graduation, and since then, both he and I have been making them this way anytime we get a chance. The sweetness of the cider is balanced by the sharp vinegar and the subtle smokiness of the smoked paprika.

For the ribs

8 large garlic cloves

1½ tablespoons kosher salt

2 tablespoons apple cider

2 tablespoons light or dark brown sugar

1 teaspoon cayenne pepper

1 teaspoon black pepper

8 pounds baby back pork ribs (eight 1-pound racks or four 2-pound racks)

1½ cups water

For the glaze

2 cups apple cider

½ cup apple cider vinegar

½ cup light or dark brown sugar

¼ teaspoon smoked paprika

¾ teaspoon kosher salt

¼ teaspoon black pepper

Marinate and roast the ribs: Mince and mash the garlic and 1 teaspoon of the salt to a paste with a chef's knife. Stir the garlic together with the cider, brown sugar, cayenne, the remaining 2½ teaspoons salt, and the pepper. Rub evenly all over the ribs. Marinate, chilled and covered, for 8 to 24 hours.

Preheat the oven to 425°F, with racks in the upper and lower thirds.

Transfer the ribs to two roasting pans. Pour ¾ cup of the water into each roasting pan and tightly cover the pans with foil. Roast the ribs, switching the position of the pans halfway through, until the meat is very tender, 1¾ to 2 hours. Remove the pans from the oven and transfer the ribs to a platter.

Make the glaze: Add 1 cup of the cider to each roasting pan and scrape up the browned bits. Skim off and discard any fat, then transfer the liquid to a large skillet. Add the vinegar, brown sugar, smoked paprika, salt, and pepper and bring to a boil, stirring occasionally. Boil until reduced to about 1 cup, about 15 minutes.

Grill the ribs: Preheat the grill.

Brush some of the glaze onto both sides of the ribs. Grill, turning occasionally, until the ribs are hot and grill marks appear, about 6 minutes. Brush the ribs with more glaze and serve the remaining glaze on the side.

Dried-Fruit-Stuffed Pork Loin with Apple-Mustard Cream serves 8 to 10

This is a festive main course, fitting for any time the family gathers together, such as Thanksgiving or Christmas. The roast is stuffed with dried fruits that play well with the pork and the creamy sauce. To make up for the lack of fat in American pork, I wrap the whole thing in bacon, which not only renders the meat moist but also adds a smoky crust and makes for a beautiful presentation.

For the stuffing

½ cup dried cranberries

½ cup chopped dried figs

½ cup dry white wine

1 onion, chopped

2 garlic cloves, finely chopped

½ stick unsalted butter

1 teaspoon finely chopped fresh thyme leaves

¾ teaspoon kosher salt

½ teaspoon black pepper

For the pork

1 (4-pound) boneless pork loin roast, trimmed of fat and silver skin

2 teaspoons kosher salt

½ teaspoon black pepper

8–10 slices bacon

Make the stuffing: Simmer the cranberries, figs, and wine together in a small heavy saucepan, covered, for 5 minutes. Remove from the heat and let the fruit steep for 10 minutes.

Cook the onion and garlic in the butter in a large heavy skillet over medium heat, stirring occasionally, until the onion begins to brown, 6 to 8 minutes. Stir in the thyme, salt, and pepper. Stir in the cranberry mixture and let the stuffing cool to room temperature.

Make the pork: Preheat the oven to 500°F.

Make a pocket in the center of the roast by inserting the end of a wooden spoon horizontally into the roast and hollowing it out, making a 1½-inch-wide tunnel. Repeat from the opposite end of the roast so the tunnel goes all the way through. Push the stuffing into the pocket from both sides, using the wooden spoon. Reserve any remaining stuffing.

Season the roast with the salt and pepper and place in a large roasting pan. Wrap the roast with the bacon, tucking the ends under the roast. Roast the pork for 20 minutes, then reduce the oven temperature to 325°F and roast until an instant-read thermometer inserted 2 inches into the center of the roast (do not touch the stuffing) registers 140°F, about 45 minutes more (1 to 1¼ hours total).

Transfer the roast to a cutting board, reserving the pan drippings, and let it stand for at least 20 minutes. (The temperature of the meat will rise to about 155°F; the meat will be moist and just slightly pink.)

½ cup dry white wine

2 Granny Smith apples, peeled, cored, and sliced ¼ inch thick

2 cups chicken stock or low-sodium broth

½ cup heavy cream

¼ cup grainy mustard

Kosher salt and black pepper

Make the sauce: Pour the pan drippings, along with any rendered fat and the juices from the cutting board, into a small heavy saucepan and add the wine and any remaining stuffing. Bring the mixture to a boil and cook until the liquid has reduced by half, about 4 minutes.

Add the apples and stock, reduce the heat to low, and simmer, stirring occasionally, until the apples are tender, about 10 minutes. Stir in the cream and mustard and simmer until the sauce is slightly thickened, 12 to 15 minutes. Season with salt and pepper to taste.

To serve, slice the roast and serve with the apple-mustard cream.

Pork and Sauerkraut serves 10

Pork, it is said, symbolizes progress, since pigs root while moving forward and their feet point forward. For this reason, pork is commonly eaten as a New Year's feast. In Pennsylvania, the pork is traditionally served with sauerkraut, a custom owing to the large German-immigrant population of the past 150 years. My family eats this dish to bring in the New Year, but it's so good that I often make it throughout the fall and winter.

4 onions, sliced

½ stick unsalted butter

2½ teaspoons kosher salt

1 cup dry white wine

2 Gala or McIntosh apples (not peeled), cored and sliced

2 pounds sauerkraut, rinsed

½ cup water

1 (8-pound) bone-in pork butt

1 teaspoon black pepper

Cook the onions in a large heavy skillet with the butter and ½ teaspoon of the salt over medium heat until they are well browned, stirring frequently as they brown, about 30 minutes. Add the wine to the skillet, scraping up any browned bits.

Preheat the oven to 350°F.

Stir the onions together with the apples, sauerkraut, and water in a large roasting pan. Rub the pork all over with the remaining 2 teaspoons salt and the pepper. Cover the pan tightly with foil and roast for 3½ hours. Uncover the pan and continue to roast until the meat is browned and falling off the bone, 30 to 40 minutes more.

Slice the meat off the bone and serve with the sauerkraut.

Orange-Lemon Escarole Salad   serves 4

I serve this unlikely showstopper as often as possible. The combination of the citrus juices, Parmesan, and escarole is unusual and totally addictive. Older escarole is best when cooked, but the young stuff (or the pale green and yellow inner leaves of the head) is mild and only slightly bitter: just add nice, salty cheese and a few squeezes of citrus, and it becomes a crisp, cool late-summer or fall salad.

1 (8-ounce) head escarole

3 tablespoons extra-virgin olive oil

1 teaspoon finely grated lemon zest

1 tablespoon lemon juice

1 tablespoon orange juice

Kosher salt and black pepper

½ cup finely grated Parmigiano-Reggiano

Remove the bitter outermost dark green leaves from the escarole. Trim and wash the pale green and yellow leaves, then tear them into bite-sized pieces.

Whisk together the oil, lemon zest, juices, and ½ teaspoon each salt and pepper, then toss with the escarole leaves. Season with salt and pepper to taste.

Sprinkle the Parmesan over the salad and serve.

Red Cabbage Balsamic Slaw with Bacon Bits and Parsley   serves 6 to 8

Hot bacon dressing makes everything better: here it helps cook the cabbage just so, taking away the raw edge. This dish is an easy way to use up a bunch of cabbage and works with almost any dinner at any time of year.

2 pounds red cabbage

8 ounces bacon, chopped

2 tablespoons extra-virgin olive oil

3 tablespoons balsamic vinegar

Kosher salt and black pepper

1 cup fresh flat-leaf parsley leaves

Quarter the cabbage, then slice it crosswise as thinly as possible with an adjustable slicer or a chef's knife.

Cook the bacon in a heavy skillet over medium heat, turning, until browned and crisp, about 7 minutes. Transfer to paper towels to cool.

Add the oil, balsamic, 1 teaspoon salt, and ½ teaspoon pepper to the skillet, scraping up any browned bits with a wooden spoon.

Toss the cabbage with the hot dressing, parsley leaves, and reserved bacon. Season with salt and pepper to taste and serve.

Chile Vinegar–Parsley Salad serves 4

When thinking about salad, don't overlook the herb garden (or the fresh herb section of the grocery store). Parsley salad, tossed with sharp vinegar, adds a welcome brightness to any rich main dish (try it with Dried-Fruit-Braised Short Ribs, page 12, or Butternut–Caramelized Onion Pizza, page 169). It also has a way of making things seem very modern and somewhat fancy with hardly any effort. If you don't have chile vinegar in your fridge, feel free to use apple cider vinegar.

3 tablespoons extra-virgin olive oil

2 tablespoons chile vinegar (page 153) or apple cider vinegar

1 small shallot, finely chopped

Kosher salt and black pepper

4 cups fresh flat-leaf parsley leaves (2 large bunches)

Whisk together the oil, vinegar, shallot, ½ teaspoon salt, and ¼ teaspoon pepper. Toss the parsley leaves with the vinaigrette just before serving. Season with salt and pepper to taste.

Fresh Ginger–Apple Tarte Tatin serves 6 to 8

This is one of my absolute favorite fall desserts, and I make it for company (or just for myself) when the apples are ready to pick. Ginger and lemon zest add a modern twist to this classic upside-down apple tart. If you're strapped for time, frozen puff pastry makes a good substitute for the pastry dough.

For the pastry dough

1¼ cups all-purpose flour

1 stick unsalted butter, cut into cubes

1 teaspoon light or dark brown sugar

½ teaspoon kosher salt

2–3 tablespoons cold water

For the filling

1½ cups sugar

2 tablespoons water

1 stick unsalted butter

1 teaspoon finely grated lemon zest

2 tablespoons lemon juice

1 tablespoon finely chopped fresh ginger

1 teaspoon ground cinnamon

¼ teaspoon freshly grated nutmeg

¼ teaspoon kosher salt

5 Winesap or Gala apples

Make the pastry dough: Work together the flour, butter, brown sugar, and salt with your hands until mostly combined, with some small lumps of butter remaining. Stir in 2 tablespoons of the water with a fork. Press a small handful of the dough together; if it looks powdery and does not come together; stir in the remaining 1 tablespoon water. Transfer the dough to a sheet of plastic wrap. Using the edge of the plastic, fold the dough over onto itself, pressing until it comes together. Form the dough into a disk, wrap completely in the plastic, and chill for 1 hour.

Meanwhile, make the filling: Heat 1 cup of the sugar with the water in a 10- to 12-inch well-seasoned cast-iron skillet (or an ovenproof nonstick skillet) over medium heat until the sugar is dissolved and bubbling, about 6 minutes. Cook the caramel, swirling the skillet occasionally, until the sugar is a dark amber caramel, 8 to 12 minutes more. Remove the skillet from the heat and add the butter, carefully swirling the skillet to incorporate the butter into the caramel. Let the caramel cool to room temperature in the skillet.

Whisk together the remaining ½ cup sugar, lemon zest, juice, ginger, cinnamon, nutmeg, and salt in a large bowl. Peel and core the apples, halve them, and toss with the sugar mixture.

Preheat the oven to 425°F, with a rack in the middle.

On a well-floured surface, roll out the pastry dough with a floured rolling pin into a 13-inch round. Place the apples, cut sides up, over the caramel in the skillet, then sprinkle with any remaining sugar mixture. Top the apples with the dough, tucking the edges of the dough down around the apples. Cut 6 steam vents in the dough.

Bake the tart until the crust is golden and the filling is bubbling, about 45 minutes.

Let the tart cool in the skillet until warm. Invert a serving plate over the skillet, then carefully reinvert the tart onto the serving plate.

Apple Rumble Crumble   serves 6

Rum and cranberries and apples and oats: this dessert was so simple that I hadn't planned on writing it down, but it was such a hit at the table that my guests wanted the recipe. (There's no crust to make, so it's a great dessert if you haven't planned ahead.) It's best to use dark rum when soaking the cranberries, but if all you have is light, use it.

For the crumble

1 stick unsalted butter, at cool room temperature

¾ cup all-purpose flour

½ cup quick-cooking oats

⅓ cup light or dark brown sugar

½ teaspoon kosher salt

For the apple rumble

½ cup dried cranberries

⅓ cup rum

5 Gala or McIntosh apples

¼ cup honey

⅓ cup sugar

2 tablespoons all-purpose flour

1 teaspoon finely grated lemon zest

Rum raisin ice cream or whipped cream for serving

Preheat the oven to 400°F, with a rack in the middle.

Make the crumble: Work together the butter, flour, oats, brown sugar, and salt with your hands until a thick dough forms (try not to overwork the crumble). Chill the crumble until you're ready to use it.

Make the apple rumble: Soak the cranberries in the rum for 30 minutes. Peel and core the apples and cut them into 1-inch chunks. Toss the apples with the honey, sugar, flour, lemon zest, and the cranberries, along with any rum that has not been absorbed. Transfer the filling to a 9-inch pie plate. Crumble the topping over the apples in mounds.

Bake until the filling is bubbling and thickened and the crumble is browned, 45 to 55 minutes. Cool slightly on a rack. Serve warm with the rum raisin ice cream or whipped cream.

Grandma McLean's Molasses Crumb Cupcakes makes 20 cupcakes

The recipe for these coffeecake-like cupcakes comes from Grandma McLean, my father's grandmother. Her original recipe called for shortening, but I prefer the flavor of butter. She used sour milk, a testament to her thrifty Scottish heritage. I use buttermilk, which lends a slight tanginess and moisture. The cupcakes are just as good for breakfast as they are for dessert.

3½ cups all-purpose flour

1 cup sugar

1½ sticks unsalted butter, at room temperature

¼ teaspoon ground cinnamon

¾ teaspoon kosher salt

2 large eggs

1 cup mild molasses

1 cup buttermilk or sour milk

1 teaspoon baking soda

¼ cup boiling water

Preheat the oven to 350°F, with a rack in the middle.

In a large bowl, work together the flour, sugar, butter, cinnamon, and salt with your hands until it looks like a crumble, with some small lumps of butter remaining. Scoop out 1 cup of the flour crumble mixture and set aside.

Add the eggs, molasses, and buttermilk to the flour mixture in the large bowl, whisking until combined. Stir the baking soda into the boiling water in a small bowl, then whisk into the batter. (You will see some small lumps of butter in the batter.)

Line 20 cupcake cups with paper liners, then fill three-quarters full with the batter. Sprinkle the reserved crumble evenly over the batter. Bake until a toothpick inserted into the center of the cupcakes comes out clean, about 20 minutes. Remove from the pan and cool on a rack before serving.

Index

Note: *Italicized* page references indicate recipe photographs.